# Edges of the State

## Forerunners: Ideas First

Short books of thought-in-process scholarship, where intense analysis, questioning, and speculation take the lead

FROM THE UNIVERSITY OF MINNESOTA PRESS

# Edges of the State

John Protevi

*University of Minnesota Press*

MINNEAPOLIS

LONDON

Published by the University of Minnesota Press, 2019
111 Third Avenue South, Suite 290
Minneapolis, MN 55401–2520
http://www.upress.umn.edu

The University of Minnesota is an equal-opportunity educator and employer.

To Kate, always.

# Contents

# Introduction: Statifications

> The state does not have an essence. The state is not a universal nor in itself an autonomous source of power. The state is nothing else but the effect, the profile, the mobile shape of a perpetual statification [*étatisation*] or perpetual statifications [*étatisations*] in the sense of incessant transactions which modify, or move, or drastically change, or insidiously shift sources of finance, modes of investment, decision-making centers, forms and types of control, relationships between local powers, the central authority, and so on.
>
> —MICHEL FOUCAULT, *The Birth of Biopolitics*

IN THE ABOVE PASSAGE, Foucault de-essentializes the state by emphasizing its processual character; it is not a thing but a modification of "governmentality" practices. (Governmentality is a mode of power; as such it is an attempt to "structure the possible field of action of others" but in the mode of "conduct of conduct" [Foucault 2000, 341], that is, leading, inducing, or incentivizing rather than commanding or terrorizing or other coercive means of shaping the field of action.) Hence, Foucault recommends we do not start by analyzing the "essence" of the state and then trying to deduce current practices of state governmentality as accidents accruing to the substance defined by that essence; rather we should look to "incessant transactions which modify" preexisting practices. Foucault continues with his nominalist antiessentialism: "The state has ... no interior. The state is nothing else but the mobile effect of a regime of multiple governmentalities" (Foucault 2008, 77).

Although in the above passage Foucault is writing about the shift in Europe from multiple feudal and religious practices to cen-

tralized administrative state functions, nonetheless we can gener-
alize the notion of "statification" as the production of state-form
social relations in any context. In this way, we can see statification
in the anthropological sense as the centralizing and hierarchizing
inherent in the putting into the state-form of social relations of
nonstate societies such as egalitarian forager bands and chief-led
autonomous villages.

The task of this book, then, is to use the generalized notion of
statification to shift perspective and, instead of looking, as almost
all political philosophers do, for the criteria by which states are
justified, look rather at the edges of statification: their breakdowns
and attempts to repair them, and their encounters with nonstate
peoples, both their predecessors and their neighbors, those who
were incorporated into states, and those who flee and fight them.

To get at what happens at the edges of the state, I call upon anthropology, political philosophy, neuroscience, evolutionary biology, child-development psychology, and other fields to look at
states as projects of constructing "bodies politic" where the civic
and the somatic intersect, where small- and large-scale social relations are made to fit with individual and group affective cognitive
structures via subjectification practices.

In my investigation of state-formation processes, I take my
ontological framework from Deleuze and Guattari and from
Manuel DeLanda. I identify multiplicities, or dynamic interact-
ing processes with critical takeoff points in multiple registers:
temporal (evolutionary, developmental, and intergenerational),
social (group dynamics, family dynamics, caretaker dynamics), and somatic (neural and endocrinological patterning). Not
only are there dynamic interactions in the processes in each of
these registers, there are loops among registers, via processes of niche construction and epigenetic inheritance discussed
in Developmental Systems Theory (Oyama, Griffiths, and Gray
2001). If we adopt the most radical interpretations of those phe-
nomena, the result of these loops is that bodies politic are constructed not only via gene–culture interaction bringing changes

to DNA sequences, but also via heritable changes to gene expression pathways provoked by socialization processes constituting historically variable niches (Protevi 2009 and 2013).

In this wide-ranging materialist ontology, I use the same basic concepts of self-organizing systems in both natural and social registers. This enables me to couple the political and the bodily, to connect the social and the somatic. Basically, Deleuze and Guattari let us go "above," "below," and "alongside" the subject: above to geo-eco-politics, below to bioculture, and alongside to socio-technical assemblages. We live at the crossroads: singular subjects arise from a crystallization or resolution of a distributed network of natural processes and social practices.

A "bodies politic" approach sees human nature as biocultural; by connecting the social and the somatic we avoid the extremes of social constructivism and genetic determinism. In a formula, human nature has evolved to be open enough to our nurture that it becomes a sort of second nature; there is, however, a default, though not failsafe, predisposition to prosociality, to being emotionally invested in social partners and patterns, to the point of bearing risks to help others and to reinforce practices. In imbricating the social and the somatic, a bodies-politic framework allows us to see that the reproduction of social systems requires producing (somatic) bodies whose affective-cognitive patterns and triggers fit the functional needs of the system. In turn, such patterning enables social systems that direct material flows. I think this allows both an emergence perspective such that social systems are emergent from constituents but are immanent to the system they form with them, and a concretion perspective such that individuals are crystallizations of systems—or more prosaically, we grow up in systems that form us.

### Forecast of Chapters

In chapter 1, "Breakdowns of the State: Prosocial Behavior in Disasters," we will find, in the breakdown of the modern state, prosocial behavior overcoming state-supported atomization. Understanding prosociality will lead us to questions about political emotion and about the evolution of altruism (aid to others with a fitness cost). If you adopt the individual as the unit of selection, then contemporary altruism is a puzzle, as traits leading to it should have been selected against. There are a number of postulated processes to solve the puzzle while still maintaining the individual as unit of selection, but if the move to rehabilitate group selection is accepted, then altruism could evolve, as fitness costs to individuals would be compensated for at the group level. But what is the selection pressure at group level? A response given by Darwin and recently re-adopted by some present-day thinkers is war. But was war prevalent enough in prestate times to serve such a role? We will take this question up in chapters 2 and 3.

In chapter 2, "Before the State: Rousseau and the *Discourse on Inequality*," I look at this beautiful text at the intersection of philosophy and anthropology, noting three points where it can be put in contact with contemporary thought. First, I examine Rousseau's "savage man" and the anthropological thesis of "human self-domestication" in the transition into, and shifts within, the genus *Homo*. Second, I look at Rousseau's "happiest and most lasting epoch"—after the "first revolution" resulted in humans living in egalitarian forager bands—in the context of the current anthropological debates about how to interpret contemporary foragers. Third, I briefly touch on Rousseau's account of the origin of cities, states, agriculture, and slavery and the current anthropological debates about the origin of war, in order to set up the work in chapters 3 and 4.

In chapter 3, "Warding Off the State: Nonstate Economies of Violence," I investigate theories that patterns (or "economies") of violence among prestate peoples had the effect of preventing state formation. Here we find the legacy of Pierre Clastres (1989 and 1994), who identified war in "primitive" society as an antistate social mechanism. But "primitive" for Clastres generalizes over quite different nonstate social formations, egalitarian nomadic foragers, and chief-led sedentary horticulturalists. They have different ways of avoiding the state; in fact, following Christopher Boehm (2012a and 2012b), we can say that the economy of violence of nomadic foragers is both antistate and antiwar. Here we will have to talk about ostracism, exile, and capital punishment as intragroup antistate economies of violence, and personalized vengeance as intergroup antiwar mechanisms.

In chapter 4, "Origins of the State: James C. Scott, Statification, and *Marronage*," I investigate, with the help of Guillaume Sibertin-Blanc (2016, Deleuze and Guattari's positing of the state-form and the primitive-form as virtual "abstract machines" incarnated in varying relations of actual state and nonstate bodies politic. I then use that framework to analyze James C. Scott's work on the "deep history" of the first Mesopotamian states, *Against the Grain* (2017), and his treatment of state and nonstate peoples in *The Art of Not Being Governed* (2009). A prime concern of Scott is maroon societies formed by people fleeing from states; according to Scott, who knowingly adopts the pejorative term states use for nonstate peoples, such "barbarians" have their own economy of violence by which—in competing with state elites—they prey upon the state's domesticated work force, the primary producers of agricultural surplus.

In chapter 5, "Fractures of the State: Deleuze and Guattari on Ideology," I investigate the social reproduction processes of states. If states are ongoing processes of statification, then the social relations that constitute them must be constantly reproduced. While ideology is supposed to explain the production and reproduction of "bodies politic," Deleuze and Guattari think ideology, qua belief structures, is not up to the task; it fails especially with fascism, as it cannot handle subpersonal body-political affective-cognitive patterning or "desire." In response, Deleuze and Guattari develop a notion of microfascism that spreads throughout a society enabling a macrofascist state. But can we save the term *ideology* by including affect? I do not see why not; it might be that Deleuze and Guattari's belief-centered notion is a straw man for certain rich concepts of ideology, which already include affect.

In the Conclusion, "Human Nature at the Edges of the State," I bring together the themes of the book to propose the following normative standard drawn from a notion of prosocial human nature: *Act such that you nurture the capacity to enact repeatable active joyous encounters of positive sympathetic care and fair cooperation for self and others without qualification.*

# 1. Breakdowns of the State: Prosocial Behavior in Disasters

The Haitian people were their own first responders.

—RUSSEL HONORÉ, CNN interview

## Disaster Politics

Let's begin with the false "security" fears that delayed and militarized the U.S. response to the Haitian earthquake (echoing the Katrina response [Protevi 2009]). Instead of rescue, relief, and security (in that temporal and priority order), the priorities of the last two were reversed and relief was delayed and subordinated to security.

There was an immense amount of media fear mongering in the aftermath of both Hurricane Katrina and the Haitian earthquake. Anarchy in the streets, food riots, "looting," sexual predation (especially prevalent after Katrina, no doubt due to the presence of "tourists"—code for "white"). But these fantasies covered over the fact that the Haitian people, like those of New Orleans, had not "descended into anarchy" but had themselves already commenced their own rescue effort; although they needed supplies for relief, they did not need to have relief trumped by "security." In the words of General Russell Honoré, of the Katrina rescue effort, the people of Haiti, like those of New Orleans, "were their own first responders" (CNN 2010). They needed relief organizations (including the military, but in a mission prioritizing relief over security) catalyzing and organizing the already activated prosocial behaviors of the Haitians; there was little need to securitize the situation.

There is very good sociological evidence from the University of Delaware Disaster Research Center (http://www.udel.edu/DRC/) that shows widespread prosocial behavior in the aftermath of disasters. The Delaware scholars also criticize the role of media in spreading "disaster myths" that include the idea of widespread antisocial behavior; these myths feed into the securitization of rescue efforts (Tierney, Bevc, and Kuligowski 2006).

The basic political-theory perspective is the following: far from showing a Hobbesian nightmare of atomized or at best gang predation in the wake of the failure of the state, the overwhelming evidence of prosocial behavior in disasters shows the fragility of the atomization practice of contemporary neoliberal capitalism. It's not that the state is needed to keep a precarious social contract together so that otherwise "naturally" atomic individuals will not prey upon each other; it's that the state is needed to enforce policies that foreclose the prosocial behavior that would otherwise emerge (Ostrom 2005) and that does in fact emerge in disasters. Delays of a few critical days can, however, produce incidents of antisocial behavior that are then, retrospectively, seen as justification for the initial "security" fears. This production of what retrospectively justifies the securitization is also seen in "kettling" maneuvers by police—or indeed just their showing up in riot gear—that produces the violence that it was supposed to prevent and thus retrospectively legitimates the kettling (Reicher et al. 2007).

Although the above is a good general framework, it needs some nuancing. Some media coverage of disasters emphasizes prosocial behavior, celebrating it as evidence of common humanity underneath "political" or "social" divisions (rarely thematized, it must be said, as "class" divisions). However, the Katrina coverage was notable for its credulity with regard to rumors (disproved within a month or so) of antisocial behavior that in retrospect were little more than shameful racial stereotypes of violent and sexually aggressive African American males. So, it often depends on whether the right kind of disaster victim is being portrayed.

## Political Emotions

Hidden by the fear mongering were instances of empathy-motivated prosocial behavior. Empathy motivates helping behavior, by pulling us to care about other people for the sake of those people. But prosociality is not "niceness"; it also motivates punishment of wrongdoers. We also need to distinguish empathy from two other sorts of feeling: (1) emotional contagion (the way emotions can spread among people, especially infants); and (2) sympathy (feeling something that someone else does). We further need to distinguish helping motivated by empathy (helping them for their sake, because they need help) from helping motivated by stress relief (helping someone to alleviate the bad feeling you have from their distress) (Stueber 2017).

There are many other prosocial emotions besides empathy: righteous indignation (shading into outright anger), shame, guilt, joy, and so on. Although the prosocial emotions are important, we should not think that prosociality has no intellectual component. Many cases of social conflict are not clear-cut and require discussion and debate. In Protevi 2009, I proposed that our concrete psychological life is affective-cognitive: all cognitive acts are emotionally shaped and inflected, while emotions have cognitive, reality-shaping and -disclosing, dimensions.

Let me say a few words about affective neuroscience treatments of fear and panic (LeDoux 1996 and 2016 Panksepp 1998 and about mirror neurons and empathy (Gallese 2001; Heyes 2010). The admittedly speculative idea I am proposing here is that fear and panic are individualizing while empathy is socializing. Although socializing empathy—obviously needing correct child-rearing practices and obviously with culturally different triggers and, to some extent, patterns—is our evolutionarily default setting (which now needs disasters to reveal itself, given atomizing neoliberal practices), atomizing panic trumps empathy via an extra affective charge in certain specific and highly intense situations (such as fire in enclosed spaces). The extra affective charge of panic makes it more attention grabbing; in other words, we are evolutionarily primed to pay more attention to panic behavior in conspecifics than to socializing empathic behavior, as that is the norm or default setting. This extra affective charge is used by media to elicit attention to reports that emphasize if not invent panic and antisocial behavior in disasters.

Whatever your position in theory of emotions, as a corporealist (Damasio 1999) or a constructivist (LeDoux 2016 or Barrett 2017), singular encounters are the genesis of emotional structures. And whatever your position in moral psychology, whether an emotion-first intuitionist or someone who accords some weight in some circumstance to moral reflection (interestingly, Jonathan Haidt [2001], although most closely identified with the former, also allows for the latter), emotions are important in analyzing bodies politic, either as generators of opinion, as obstacles to proper judgment, or as indicators of virtue or vice.

Corporealism also doesn't fit with constructivist theories, which will insist on the contribution of semantic factors, as in the radical theory of Lisa Feldman Barrett or the more modest constructivism of Joseph LeDoux. LeDoux's constructivism is moderate in comparison to Barrett (2017), insofar as he does allow some reference to specific subcortical defense reactive circuits that are added to other inputs in his "recipe" for fear (LeDoux 2016 93–112). Barrett, however, insists on a strong neural globalism, which, with her insistence on holism, emergence, and degeneracy (same outcome from different mechanisms), results in a strong nominalism, such that no "fingerprint" of necessary circuits can be identified for either emotion instances or even emotion categories (2017, 35–41).

For Barrett, emotion occurs when an emotion concept is unpacked. For her, emotion-concept construction occurs via learning, that is, a bottom-up summarizing of singular experiences, drawing on neural inputs from multiple brain sites mapping the body and other higher and lower intrabrain regions; each of these experiences is tagged with culturally specific emotion terms.

Hence there is a high-level, cortical/semantic component to concepts, which are constructed from these multiple inputs. Such summarizing produces concepts as abstract but nonessential capacities that do not exist as enduring, locatable, actual firings but only insist as potentials for actualization. Given her strong holism, emergence, and degeneracy, concept creation is the progressive construction of a virtual field: virtual, because concepts do not exist in actuality but insist in potentiality.

An emotional episode is an instance of a concept, that is, the actualization of the potential concept. It occurs as prediction, a top-down simulation that "unpacks" concepts. Such unpacking constructs an instance of the concept that assembles its components from occurrent inputs and checks the assemblage against the prediction. This actualization occurs in a degeneracy mode, such that no single set of neural firings is necessary for each instance of the concept. Hence the concept is a virtual diagram with multiple mechanisms for the actualization of instances. In Deleuzean terms, it is an "abstract machine" with multiple machinic assemblages for its actualization.

This is not all that different from the corporealists if we allow for cortical brain firings to count as "states of the body" (the brain is part of the body, in a certain sense, if "body" is thought as the "material occasion for emotional events" rather than as "outside-the-brain but up to and including the skin"). Where does that body state come from? From the history of encounters of the body, that is, from the interaction of the particular character of the body and the objects (people and things) it encounters. The history of encounters patterns the body by modulating its characteristic responses, deepening the affective response upon repetition of similar objects; that is, in Barrett's terms, experience generates more and more deeply embedded and finely grained emotional concepts.

Here the brain/body is not a blank slate nor a preformed set of responses. Encounters are not imprintings nor are they mere triggers; rather, the body politic has characteristic dispositions that set up a range of stylized responses. Similarly, this is not a nominalist position of sheer idiosyncratic—and hence unpredictable—responses; nor is it a universalist human nature in which we can predict responses. Rather, if we get to know someone, and see an encounter with a relatively familiar object, we have a good sense of what will happen. But bodies are complex, and internal changes arise, as do situations unfamiliar to the agent, such that predictions of the response are less reliable, both to the onlookers and even to the experiencing agent: we can surprise ourselves with changes in our emotional patterns.

From the importance of encounters flows the importance of institutions. If one can set up ways in which some patterns of encounters can be made more likely than others, one can influence brain/bodily histories, and thus emotional responses, and thus the impulses toward moral action (whatever you think of the efficacy of later rational reflection). When people live in a society with firmly set institutions, their brain/bodies, intuitions, emotions, and impulses toward actions are more or less predictable, and, if the institutions are well attuned to each other, social reproduction occurs more smoothly than if the institutions clash.

### Evolution of Altruism

Determining how we got to the point where there is still empathetic horizontal prosociality enabling altruism able to peak through in breakdowns of the state is only a problem for evolutionary biologists who adopt a gene-for-trait development model, and for game theory behavioral individualists in which avoiding exploitation by detecting and then punishing (thus bearing a fitness cost) free riders and bullies ("egoists") is the selection pressure. Those bringing to bear ethnography of forager bands (e.g., Boehm 2012b or Sterelny 2012) will say it's not hard to detect free riding or bullying so that social selection is less a cognitive problem than one of action coordination.

It is common to distinguish three forms of altruism: the psychological, which involves the intent to help others; the moral, which involves the intent to help others with no thought of return; and the evolutionary, which involves fitness-hurting action for non-kin (Kitcher 2011).

Explaining the evolution of altruism is a problem if one assumes a gene or individual-level selection, since carriers of altruism-enabling traits would have been selected against. Recall the formula for natural selection: variation of fitness-affecting heritable traits in a population whose environment exerts a selection pressure favoring organisms with some traits, resulting in a difference in traits in succeeding generations. Now, Darwin did not have the notion of "gene," though he did have a postulated inheritance mechanism ("gemmule"). It is only with recovery of Mendel's work that genes were postulated as inheritance markers. After solving the problem of continuous variation in a population, the "Modern Synthesis" wed natural selection and population genetics. Watson and Crick (and Franklin) provided our understanding of the molecular structure of DNA, positing it as the physical structure of genes regulating inheritance and development as in the so-called Molecular Revolution and its "Central Dogma" (for a brief history, see Keller 2000).

Although many thinkers are satisfied with explanations of the evolution of altruism at individual-level selection (e.g., Sterelny 2012 and 2014; Tomasello 2016), some other recent thinkers have advocated a return to explaining altruism with the concept of group selection (Sober and Wilson 1998). We'll look specifically at the questions about the role of war and group selection for altruistic or at least prosocial behavior and emotion.

Altruism is helping behavior with a fitness cost. "Fitness" in evolutionary terms is measured by the number of descendants living to reproductive age. Fitness cost can be as dramatic as self-sacrifice, but also just time spent away from mate selection, child raising, resource provision, and so on. This includes prosocial and third-party punishment as they carry risks: you could start a feud; you eliminate a potential ally. Prosocial behavior is then helping and hurting others according to social patterns. Thus, "prosocial" doesn't mean "nice"; it means an intellectual understanding of, and emotional investment in, social partners and patterns, which can motivate and justify punishing violators as well as helping those in need.

Scholars have proposed several ways of explaining helping behavior that appears to be altruistic but has hidden benefits that balance out (or outweigh) the fitness costs: (1) kin selection: costly helping behavior that helps genes in kin to survive ("I would sacrifice myself for two brothers or for eight cousins"); (2) reciprocal altruism: aid given back to donor by recipient with time delay ("I'll scratch your back if you scratch mine"); (3) mutualism: working together so that immediate benefits (at end of successfully completed task) accrue to all parties compensating for any costs; (4) indirect altruism: aid given by an altruist with an eye to payback by a third party due to reputation gained by altruistic acts; and (5) sexual selection (qua female mate preference instead of male arms race): altruist behavior as "costly signaling," hence as predictor of genetic quality.

Social selection (Boehm 2012a and b) is behavior enforcing egalitarianism; it takes the form of ridicule, exile, or killing. Often it is the kin of the mad dog or simple bully prone to violence who step in to take him out, to prevent escalation. Here we see the origin of conscience as self-inhibitor of temptations to nonsharing and active theft, bullying, killing, and so on ("You better think twice, because if you make a mistake the group is going to react harshly").

### War as Selection Pressure for Altruism

This passage on altruism, group selection, and warfare from Darwin's 1871 *The Descent of Man* is very widely quoted.

> When two tribes of primeval man, living in the same country, came into competition, if (other things being equal) the one tribe included a great number of courageous, sympathetic and faithful members, who were always ready to warn each other of danger, to aid and defend each other, this tribe would succeed better and conquer the other. (Darwin 2004 [1871], 113)

Several new works (e.g., Bowles and Gintis 2011) take up Darwin's suggestion and posit widespread prestate war as a necessary selection pressure for prosocial behavior, calculations, and emotions. Fry 2013 will challenge them, asking whether war was prevalent enough for it to be the selection pressure for altruism. Three scientific fields provide the questions here: biology, archeology, and ethnography. Biology asks about the relation of anonymous group violence in humans to group raiding in chimpanzees. Archaeology asks whether the archeological record supports the hypothesis of prevalent prestate war. And ethnography asks how studies of contemporary nomadic forager bands can help us hypothesize whether prestate social structures and eco-social conditions were consistent with prevalent warfare.

To follow up on these issues, I turn in chapter 2 to Rousseau, whose *Discourse on Inequality* provides a framework for discussing the place of war in human evolution.

## 2. Before the State: Rousseau and the *Discourse on Inequality*

> Thus, although men now had less endurance, and natural pity had already undergone some attenuation, this period in the development of human faculties, occupying a just mean between the indolence of the primitive state and the petulant activity of our amour propre, must have been the happiest and the most lasting epoch.
>
> —ROUSSEAU, *Discourse on Inequality*

HOBBES, LOCKE, AND ROUSSEAU all look to empirical accounts of human behavior from their own time, from history, and from travelers' accounts of foreign lands to ground their theories of human nature. Thus, they are all naturalists of a sort; for them political philosophy must be constrained by the type of beings we are; for them there's no use in creating a system of justice that could not be instantiated here on this earth with its inhabitants.

While Hobbes and Locke appeal to history and travel accounts to provide depth and breadth to the evidence for their notion of human nature, it's remarkably static; the accounts they adduce go to show that humans are basically the same, with the observed variation being reasonable adaptation to circumstances. So, it's not really Rousseau's appeals to history and to far-off lands that set him apart from Hobbes and Locke; rather it's his appeal to the qualitative shifts in the development of human nature that counts, and that marks his modernity.

We would now, since the famous phrase of Lévi-Strauss (1977)—"Rousseau, founder of the human sciences"—think of

Rousseau at the intersection of anthropology and political philosophy. In this chapter, I will note three points where the *Discourse on Inequality* provides food for thought about the possibilities of such an intersection. I will first consider Rousseau's "savage man" and the anthropological thesis of "human self-domestication" in the transition into and within the genus *Homo*. Next I will look at Rousseau's "happiest and most lasting epoch" after the "first revolution," resulting in humans living in acephalic egalitarian nomadic forager bands; here we will consider the anthropological debates about how to interpret contemporary foragers. And third, I will consider Rousseau's account of the origin of cities, states, agriculture, and slavery and the current anthropological debates about the origin of war.

### "Savage Man"

Following Wokler (2012), we can interpret much of what Rousseau says about the "freedom," "perfectibility," "self-love" (*amour de soi-même*), and "pity," of "savage man" as describing a hypothetical primate endowed with the potentials for human aptitudes that only begin to be fully actualized after the "first revolution," which leads to the true sociability of humans in early forager bands. Wokler 2012 looks to Rousseau's mentions of contemporary accounts of the behavior of orangutans. Insofar as Rousseau thought that those apes might actually be part of the human species, for him they might be examples of "savage man."

What Rousseau describes as human freedom from animal instincts would be seen in contemporary terminology as developmental neural and behavioral plasticity (Wexler 2006): with the exception of startle reflexes, patterns of defensive physiological reaction, and some strong tendencies to easily acquired fear of snakes and cliffs, humans are remarkably open to learning responses to even dangerous situations. While fast messages from sense organs activate defensive reactions, parallel cortical evaluations arrive very soon afterward and can provide a choice from a range of learned maneuvers (LeDoux 2016). It's that addition of cortical evaluation that frees us from what looks like the automated reactions of other animals. (The burgeoning fields of animal cognition studies, some of which are summarized in Barrett 2011, show that many animals also have a range of reactions so that one is more or less "chosen" from a repertoire given their own evaluations of sensory stimuli; hence rather than emphasizing the fixity of animal "instincts," we can instead emphasize the qualitatively greater human evaluative and choice capacities.)

Such plasticity is the condition for what Rousseau calls "perfectibility," the capacity to develop a ratcheting effect of needs, passions, and reason: new needs bring new desires, which awaken reason to search for solutions, which in turn become needs as our bodies and minds become "addicted" to those cultural mechanisms (Henrich 2016). In contemporary terms, we talk of niche construction or obligatory scaffolding or cultural learning. A physiological example: our ability to cook meat means we have offloaded a good bit of our digestion, shortening our intestines, shrinking our canine teeth, and expanding the range of foods we can handle (Wrangham 2009). Henrich (2016) demonstrates this point with stories of the failure of stranded European explorers unless they adopted native ways in food identification and preparation.

Let's recall Rousseau's relation of self-love and pity in savage man. For Rousseau, as savage man has very few relations with other humans, the self-preservation of one rarely impinges on that of another. Thus, for Rousseau it was Hobbes's illegitimate importation of the need to assuage the socially developed passions of pride and security into the condition of savage man that led him astray. Being ignorant of such vices, and having few needs and passions, leads to the "goodness" qua nonwickedness of savage man.

That's not to say that for Rousseau there were never occasions for conflict among men; it's here however that he invokes pity as another counterpoint to Hobbes. We both look out for our survival and feel an immediate repugnance at the pain of another.

There are three aspects contemporary thinkers would distinguish in Rousseau's account of pity (Stueber 2017). The first would be "emotional contagion," in which emotions spread from one organism to another, as in the wave of panic sweeping through a crowd. The second would be empathy, or "commiseration," which is, as Rousseau notes, strengthened by identification. This would be when one feels what the other is feeling. Contemporary thought warns here of in-group versus out-group effects and the way in which acting to help a suffering person can involve self-care; you are acting in part to reduce the pain you feel. A third aspect is "sympathy," which involves understanding the emotional state of others without necessarily feeling that state and being moved to help them for their own sakes. (For my part, pure "sympathy" is a limit case; it seems true to experience that empathy and sympathy are blended in concrete cases.)

The next thing we have to talk about here is that Rousseau's model of "savage man," the orangutans, are solitary, and what we now know of our evolution doesn't indicate a transition from solitary living to social life, but a growth from the social lives of our last common ancestor (LCA) to the split between the lineage that becomes *Pan* (which now includes chimpanzees and bonobos) and the lineage that becomes *Homo* (now represented by modern humans). Comparative work looks to reconstruct an LCA from behaviors appearing in all descendants, even those undergoing considerable change since the split. As current *Pan* and *Homo* creatures are social, we can conclude the LCA was as well. But the type of sociality it exhibits is a matter of controversy.

Chimpanzees have lots of intermale aggression, hierarchy and male alliances, tolerated food scrounging, and opportunistic ambush killing of neighbors in border zones. Bonobos have female alliances suppressing male coalitions, little intermale fighting, use of sex in various combinations for conflict avoidance and resolution, and no border ambushes. If the LCA was more chimpanzee-like than bonobo-like, then evolutionary human emotional development (one example of the study of which is the "human self-domestication" thesis or HSD) is mostly about cortical anger and aggression control of emotions oriented to domination. But if there were significant bonobo traits, we would have developed capacities for top-down anger control as well as capacities for bottom-up pacific emotions. But if we remain agnostic about the LCA—that is, even if we don't adopt the position that there were significant bonobo-like traits in the LCA—we might have developed capacities for bottom-up pacific emotions (joy in cooperation, helping, and caring) at the same time as those for top-down anger control. I don't have the training to make a real call here, but as a philosopher I can describe the implications of adopting one position or another, and agnosticism about the LCA would indicate plasticity and independent evolution of specific chimp, bonobo, and human traits.

When circumstances permit, humans are remarkably pacific and sharing. Is this because we have learned ways to suppress our dominance-enabling, hair-trigger temper and violent reactive aggression? Or is it because we genuinely and positively have an emotional structure that provides pleasure in peace and sharing? Well, for most people most of the time it's a little bit of both. It's not impossible to find pure examples of bullies and saints (and current politics seems to reward bullies, who might be expressing a developmental switch in a norm of reaction model that produces a behavior set adapted to circumstances of violent uncertainty), but it's relatively rare (Gonzalez-Cabrera 2017; Vaesen 2014).

So, when they do take hold, is peace and sharing something we have to internalize as a result of learning that they pay off relative to the risk/reward calculation our environment presents? Or is it something that, given the appropriate environment, is nurtured from an already-internal seed? One interesting clue is the "overjustification effect" in which otherwise intrinsically motivated child helping is hurt by the presence of external reward (Tomasello 2016; Warneken and Tomasello 2008). The children in these experiments do not want to keep helping because of a cookie they might get; they want to play because helping is pleasurable.

**The Long Happy Epoch**

We now turn to the transition from Rousseau's hypothetical reconstruction of savage man in the primary state of nature—the superabundant "forest"—to the discussion of human life in the "happiest and the most lasting epoch," after the catastrophe-induced formation of "nascent society" but before the formation of states, agriculture, slavery, and war. As there never were solitary primates in our line, nor was there ever a time without the sort of ecological "accidents" Rousseau invokes as the cause of our coming together, what we see here is the opportunity to discuss human evolution, specifically, as befits a chapter on Rousseau, the development of modern human emotional structures.

This emotional development occurred in a time of the transition to obligate collective foraging (Tomasello 2016). We cannot consider contemporary foragers to be "living fossils" as many of Rousseau's formulations seem to suggest. (While Rousseau never claims that contemporary nonstate peoples are fully "savage man" in the sense of never having departed the "first state of nature," he does say that the Caribs "have deviated least from the state of Nature" [Rousseau 1997, 156].)

However, while it might be possible to carefully consider ethnographies of their social life as part of a reconstruction of early human foragers, we cannot make Rousseau's unqualified assumption that contemporary foragers are "closer" to early bands. A number of issues arise here. First, it is increasingly difficult to find people who haven't had dealings with states and their agents or to find people whose neighbors deal with them on the basis of their own dealings with states. Second, geographical circumscription by states will tend to push contemporary foragers to lands whose exploitation by states is more difficult than just letting the foragers occupy them for the time being, whether or not the foragers would prefer other territories; the contemporary necessity of food production on the marginal lands to which they are confined might very well have led to significant changes in forager behavior relative to earlier, pre-state times. Third, and in particular, state-led geographical circumscription might lead to two problems: (a) the loss of group fission as a form of intragroup conflict resolution, and (b) the loss of group flight as a form of intergroup conflict avoidance. The loss of these options might then have led to increased intra- and intergroup violence relative to pre-state peoples. No one proposes a time in which humans did not engage personal violence; what is disputed is the ease with which one extrapolates from contemporary data to pre-state times; it is here that bitter debates around archeological findings spring up (Ferguson 2013a; Widerquist and McCall 2016).

All this is related to one of the most interesting new discussions in contemporary anthropology, the "human self-domestication" (HSD) thesis. For Hare (2017), the HSD "also led to enhanced cooperation in intergroup conflicts." We have to nuance this claim, however, by delving into the various "economies of violence" that inform debates on the origin of war (see chapter 3). Here the basic question is whether war is a universal human experience, or whether it only occurs in certain social circumstances. The key distinction, in my mind, is that proposed by Raymond Kelly (2000; 2005) between vengeance as personal and war as anonymous. If you define war as anonymous intergroup violence, the case can be made that it only arises in segmented societies, leaving unsegmented forager societies as those without war, and thus defeating the universal war thesis. (See Fry 2013 for a full treatment of the issue.)

To see what's going on here, note that a prime selection pressure for self-domestication in early humans is capital punishment in unsegmented foragers (Wrangham 2014; the success or failure of capital punishment in reducing murder in state societies is not directly deducible from its use in early forager societies). There is an interesting dialectic here: the egalitarian or "acephalic" social structure of forager bands is produced by the capital punishment of murderers qua would-be dominators, while that same structure produces the need for capital punishment, as, without an alpha to impose conflict resolution, individual conflict can result in murder, and hence the need for capital punishment (Boehm 2012b). Forager capital punishment is a paradigm case of "warm" proactive aggression (Wrangham 2014), but the targeted killers are those hotheads exhibiting poor control of reactive aggression or those cold-blooded bullies whose instrumental aggression is used to dominate others. Capital punishment thus selects for the ability to carry out the controlled anger / proactive aggression complex that enables war: it is language-mediated, group-oriented, and premeditated, though sometimes achieved by taking advantage of spontaneous opportunity. This would tend to be one-on-one. Note that Kelly (2000) distinguishes single capital punishment from ambush by multiple people, which would be on the way to social substitutability and war, as it requires group vengeance duty. Once we couple group duty on the side of the victimized avengers to group liability on the side of the offenders, we have set up feud, a form of war as anonymous intergroup violence.

### The Second Revolution

Rousseau's positing of a historical origin of warfare, tied to states, agriculture, and slavery, brings us to debates about the evolution of altruism. As we have seen, Darwin posited war as a selection pressure, at the group level, for altruism in pre-state societies. If one denies the existence of pre-state warfare, however, and instead places it—as does Rousseau—at the origin of agricultural states, then other means for the evolution of altruism must be proposed. Despite some of Hare's (2017) formulations, I do not think capital punishment is a form of war, even if it helps prepare for it; it is personal and intragroup as opposed to anonymous and intergroup.

An interesting new book by Samuel Bowles and Hubert Gintis, *A Cooperative Species* (2011), posits widespread pre-state war as a necessary selection pressure for prosocial behavior, calculations, and emotions. For Bowles and Gintis, the mechanisms of kin selection, mutualism, and direct and indirect reciprocity (discussed above in chapter 1) are not enough for the evolution of prosocial behaviors, calculations, and emotions. For them, war is also necessary to group selection for prosociality. Although Fry (2013a, 9–10 and 15–20) has a number of criticisms of Bowles and Gintis, it should be said that he—correctly—does not accuse them of upholding a hardcore line that human nature is that of a killer ape. Indeed, Bowles and Gintis insist that early bands had extensive trade, marriage, and generally peaceful nonconflict relations with other groups (e.g., big seasonal meetings of many bands) as well as allowing for climate disasters to be a major predictor of warfare (thus not some "aggression" thesis).

What complicates things for Bowles and Gintis is the bitter controversy in anthropology about the alleged universality of warfare in human evolution and history (Fry 2013b covers the basics from an antiuniversalist perspective). There are three elements to consider here: the archaeological, the biological, and the ethnographic. We will deal with the first two here and reserve the third for chapter 3.

Regarding the archeological: Proponents of universal war often point to findings of crushed skulls and the like in the archaeological record (Keeley 1997). Critics reply that some of the claims of war-damaged skulls are more plausibly accounted for by animal attacks (Fry 2007, 43). The antiuniversalists will also seek to demonstrate that the universalists have cherry-picked their evidence (see Ferguson 2013a and 2013b). For Ferguson, there just aren't that many (or any) pre-state multibody graves with violent marks on the skeletons. You need multibody sites because no one denies individual killing, either the murder or the "capital punishment" group response.

Regarding the biological, an important first step is to distinguish human war from chimpanzee male coalition and aggressive hierarchy, to which it is assimilated in the "humans as killer apes" hypothesis (see Ferguson 2014 for an argument that chimpanzee intergroup violence is due to human impact rather than being an adaptation). Since, as we know, bonobos and chimpanzees have different social structures and behavioral repertoires, researchers have triangulated human, chimpanzee, and bonobos (for an interesting attempt to show that the last common ancestor here was more bonobo-like than chimp-like, see Gonzalez-Cabrera 2017).

We need to include them here to tackle the "deep roots" theory of human warfare (Wrangham 1999). Chimpanzees engage in border raids, ambushing members of neighboring bands who are caught too close to the border. Wrangham categorizes chimpanzee raiding as "coalitionary violence," to which he assimilates human warfare. Ferguson (2014) denies a deep evolutionary root for chimpanzee violence (hence rupturing the "deep roots" account of human warfare) and proposes instead a Human Impact Thesis (basically territorial infringement) to account for contemporary evidence of chimpanzee intergroup raids.

Another biological issue concerns our relationship to the relatively peaceful bonobos, the other extant species in the *Pan* genus. Frans De Waal (2006) points out, against the thesis of a biological continuity of "war" from chimpanzees to humans, that bonobos are just as genetically related to us as chimpanzees. Wrangham and Peterson (1996) point to female coalition building in bonobo society as preventing intergroup violence by male coalitions. I would like to propose that the focus on eco-social difference is not going to be male bonding (chimpanzees and men) versus female bonding (bonobos) but nomadic egalitarian foragers versus hierarchical sedentary horticulturalists and agriculturalists (bands versus chiefdoms and states).

In my view, Wrangham and Peterson equivocate between "war" and "violence" (war is a very specific form of violence) and conflate "war" and "border raid"—which they in turn assimilate too quickly to chimpanzee coalitionary killing (Kelly 2005). They are right that we have to look to an eco-social multiplicity, but they overlook "techno" as one dimension, a key point of Kelly (2005), who evokes an era of defensive advantage in pre-state forager life due to the adoption of javelins as hunting and fighting weapons;

such projectile weaponry, along with knowledge of the terrain, would inflict crippling damages on invaders (see also Sterelny 2014). In sum, Wrangham and Peterson are not sufficiently careful in examining the economies of violence in different forms of human social organization. Specifically, they do not investigate egalitarian forager societies (whose antiwar practices include peace-seeking festivals) because for them all stories of antiwar societies are myths, not ethnography.

So, while Rousseau locates gruesome vengeance in the economy of violence of forager bands in "nascent society"—the beginnings of *amour propre* turn injury into insult (Rousseau 1997, 166)—he doesn't allow war until after states, and that's the point of our discussion in chapters 3 and 4.

# 3. Warding Off the State: Nonstate Economies of Violence

> Violence is found everywhere, but under different regimes and economies.
>
> —DELEUZE AND GUATTARI, *A Thousand Plateaus*

IN THE THIRTEENTH CHAPTER of *A Thousand Plateaus,* "7000 BC: Apparatus of Capture," Deleuze and Guattari write of the differences among states, "primitive" societies, and what they melodramatically call the "war machine," by invoking the concept of a "regime" or "economy" of violence (Deleuze and Guattari 1987, 425; 447–48). This would be the pattern of violence of a particular social system: under what conditions and with what frequency do individual and groups typically act violently, and with what typical responses by individuals and groups? Deleuze and Guattari intend the generalization literally: all social processes (groups are always constituted by processes with varying ratios of centripetal and centrifugal effects) have an economy of violence.

But what is "violence" in this formulation? To take a contemporary example, in *Foucault, Politics, and Violence,* Johanna Oksala defines violence in a "very narrow" manner as "intentional bodily harm that reflects the sense in which violence is generally held to be categorically objectionable" (2012, 8–9). I think this focus on bodily harm is a bit too narrow for our purposes of considering social group norm enforcement; hence I think shunning, ostracism, and exile should be included as forms of "social violence." Specifically, I want to include the social violence forms as they are a key to the antistate and antiwar effects of the economy of violence of pre-state and nonstate societies (Boehm 2012b).

This focus on nonstate societies will be a departure from Oksala and almost the entirety of contemporary political philosophy and political theory, which—after a few *pro forma* nods to the anarchist tradition—almost always looks at the economies of violence of concern to states as that which holds the monopoly on the legitimate use of violence: crimes, wars, and terrorism, matched by police, armed forces, and security forces. "What justifies what level of state violence?" is the question for these fields. That's not to say that "security studies," as a branch of the political science subfield of "International Relations," doesn't tackle the complexity of what is variously called "4GW" or "fourth-generation warfare," "post-Westphalian conflicts," and so on, but even those for the most part look at how states deal with that which escapes their control, threatens their economy of violence, and so on.

The first step away from an exclusive focus on the economies of violence of established states is to look at the economy of violence inherent in what the Introduction sketched as the Foucauldian notion of the "statification" of social organization practices. Not all societies are states, though all exercise power as a way in which certain actions may "structure the possible field of action of others" (Foucault 2000, 341). That is, all societies work at the rendering predictable of human action by institutions of external reward and punishment as well as the setting up of internal affective-cognitive patterns in "subjectification" practices. It is precisely the fact that social forms are wider than the state that allows statification. Simply as a social process, then, "statification," either in Foucault's European postfeudal context or in the anthropological sense of the putting into state-form of nonstate societies, has an economy of violence. Some societies ward off the state through their economy of violence, but those economies of violence are not necessarily that of war, as Pierre Clastres (1989; 1994) supposes. Thus, not all antistate violence is physical (ostracism and exile), nor is it organized as war (personalized vengeance is an antiwar as well as an antistate practice).

To return one last time to Oksala as our starting point, she wants to carve out a space for historical analyses of the "rationality" of economies of violence; she thereby calls on us to discard ontological and instrumental theories of violence. I agree that instrumental theories, which make violence a mere means to independently decided political ends, render us incapable of analyzing economies of violence. An economy of violence includes instrumental violence, but, in being tied in with economies of production and distribution, should also include the structural violence of malnutrition or disease from hyperexploitation (Scott 2017).

I also agree with Oksala that ontological theories, which include conceptual articulation—seeing this as that—are too broad, when they are used to ground political violence in the very nature of discursive thought. Oksala includes anthropological theories under the ontological category, meaning those that make violence an essential attribute of humans, grounded in some idea of "aggression"; I agree these are to be rejected, as similarly incapable of analyzing economies of violence, though I will do so precisely on anthropological grounds. Boehm (2012b), whom we will discuss later regarding the economy of violence of nomadic forager bands, posits a "social selection" process here. Exile and killing of overly aggressive types would allow the gene-level evolution of altruism to work. If so, then the puzzle about the evolution of altruism seen in many mathematical models would be solved as social selection would have been able to tip the scales toward the accumulation of altruistic genes.

On a methodological level, then, Boehm (2012b) is of interest for demanding that the anthropological study of the social selection practices of egalitarian forager bands be taken into account when analyzing the mathematical models that propose that the evolution of altruism is puzzling. Let me note that a current in contemporary biological anthropology mostly avoids gene-for-a-trait evolutionary models (Welsch, Vivanco, and Fuentes 2017; Fuentes 2013; Marks 2010). From the perspective of work on epigenetics and development (Griffiths and Stotz 2013; Jablonka and

Lamb 2005), social selection can also be seen as eliminating child-development practices that would set in place gene-expression networks allowing free-riding behavior by setting conscience kick-in levels lower. (That's of course if free-riding or aggressive dominance needs something as fancy as gene-expression networks and is not just learned opportunistic behavior.)

### Deleuze and Guattari on "Regimes of Violence"

The economy of violence of statification is invisible from within successfully formed state assemblages, which, in good Weberian fashion, present the force employed by state agents as legitimate protection of victims from violence coming from recalcitrant factors inside or outside the state, that is, criminals or barbarians. To render the violence of statification visible, it is necessary to see how it is "pre-accomplished," as Deleuze and Guattari put it (1987, 447–48).

Deleuze and Guattari begin by sketching Marx's analysis of capitalism as resting on violence that necessarily operates through the state but that precedes the capitalist mode of production and constitutes "primitive accumulation" or proletarianization as the removal of access to the means of production for some, thereby forcing wage labor upon them. Primitive accumulation is a violence accomplished in other modes of production, producing the proletarian and the owner, who then step onto the capitalist stage already formed and ready to play their roles. Hence the violence of primitive accumulation is difficult to pinpoint in capitalism; it is "pre-accomplished" elsewhere, though reactivated every day (as we will see in chapter 5).

Deleuze and Guattari enlarge upon Marx's analysis to put it at the origin of the state as well as operating in capitalism: primitive accumulation at the origin of the state does not arise from agriculture but precedes it. Deleuze and Guattari enunciate a general principle: there is primitive accumulation wherever an "apparatus of capture" is installed (1987, 447). (An "apparatus of capture" occurs whenever a social organization can produce comparison of abstract quantities and appropriation of surplus. In the case of the first states, Deleuze and Guattari write, the quantities are those of rent based on land productivity, labor based on regulated human activity, and taxes based on monetary flows [1987, 443–44].) The violence of primitive accumulation qua statification is thus the very constitution of the apparatus of capture: it is the violence directed at nonstate peoples that constitutes those whom it is directed against (the "cheats," "vagabonds," "criminals," "smugglers" . . . who refuse rent, labor, and taxation). In concrete terms, nonstate people (who, as we will see in chapter 4, might have pastoralism or multicrop agriculture along with foraging in complex mixtures) have to be conquered by the primary violence of statification to turn them into the primary producers—whether taxed peasants, debt bondsman, or chattel slaves—whom the tax collectors and police and army can target as cheater, delinquent, criminal, heretic, runaway in the secondary violence of the lawful mundane reactivation of statification. (Scott [2017] does allow for some voluntary joining of states, but Deleuze and Guattari [1977 and 1987] are quite consistent in emphasizing conquest as the primary mechanism for statification.)

Deleuze and Guattari (1987, 447–48) go on to distinguish four "regimes of violence"; this quick sketch will be our guide in the rest of this chapter and in chapter 4. It is important to see these as "topologically" distinct regimes of violence, not steps in an evolution from savagery to civilization. They are virtual "diagrams," which coexist on a plane of immanence; history is that concatenation of contingent circumstances that transform such virtual coexistence into actual succession (1987, 430). The four regimes are "struggle" [*lutte*], "war," "crime," and "lawful violence." Struggle [*lutte*] is the violence of nonstate or "primitive" societies. As we will see, Deleuze and Guattari elide the difference between nomadic foragers and sedentary horticulturalists; the former practice what Boehm (2012a) calls a "reverse dominance hierarchy" that prevents purely dominant individuals (so-called alphas), while the latter practice "primitive war" as "a certain ritualization of violence" as analyzed by Clastres (1989). War simpliciter for Deleuze and Guattari refers to the practices of the steppe nomads and their "war machine," which directs violence against the state. Crime is the violence of illegality or capture without self-bestowed "right"—the scare quotes here allowing us to compare barbarian raiding as an alternate form of predation on primary producers as opposed to self-created "legitimate" state taxation. State policing or lawful violence, then, has both "originary" and "secondary" aspects: it is capture simultaneously constituting the right to capture.

The earliest attempts at statification then involve the incorporation of foragers or autonomous villages and their territories into imperial legal and administrative systems. (The empire operates a "deterritorialization" in which land becomes "striated"—instead of foragers spreading out over the earth, the land is surveyed and people are assigned to plots of land—and an "overcoding" in which local customs are fit into a centralized system.) Insofar as statification creates what it is used against, state lawful violence "always seems to presuppose itself" (Deleuze and Guattari 1987, 448). Thus, a state can say violence is natural (or, echoing a certain Hobbesian logic, that the state of nature is a state of war), so it uses violence against the (naturally) violent primitives or (steppe) nomads in order that peace may reign. But the state's peace is a regime of violence that disavows itself, that structurally hides the primary violence of statification qua the primitive accumulation that denies access to the earth to nonstate people, forcing them into peasantry, debt bondage, or outright slavery; that is, those against whom secondary state violence as lawful policing of the rights of capture (rent, corvée labor, and tax collection) is then used against.

With this forecast in mind, I will examine nonstate economies of violence in the rest of this chapter, and the economy of violence of the first state-events in chapter 4.

## Nomadic Forager Bands

There is no teleology here in discussing processes that ward off or instantiate statification; states are not the "mature" form of social life and nonstate societies possess their own positivity in mechanisms for warding off state formation. Even as they have for the most part abandoned unilinear "evolutionary" theories of social "stages" (Widerquist and McCall 2017 provides a brief overview), anthropologists would still acknowledge that the nomadic forager band is the social form for the vast majority of human life, prior to the institution of the state. (In chapter 4 we will see how Scott synthesizes new research that calls into question any notion of a "Neolithic Revolution" that simultaneously—or even quickly and necessarily—brought together states, urbanism, and agriculture as a clean break from foraging.) Despite current research showing more variability than previously acknowledged among currently living foragers (Kelly 2013), we can cautiously speculate that pre-state nomadic forager bands were most likely egalitarian or "acephalic"; that they practiced "fission-fusion" and frequent inter-band visiting, rendering group identity fluid; that they often had a gendered division of labor, though with little specialization within genders; and that while there was most likely a prestige gradient relative to prowess, group discussion was the decision-making process; hence, while there was rhetoric and persuasion, there was no top-down command (Kelly 2000; Boehm 2012b; Sterelny 2014).

According to Boehm (2012b), the nomadic forager economy of violence has an antistate effect by preventing centralized power of the would-be alpha or dominating "head." Boehm is an expert in the ethnography of contemporary nomadic foragers. He cautions against the "living fossil" view, though he attempts cautious extrapolation to pre-state social existence. The forager economy of violence focuses on intragroup personal violence. Here we find individual acts of fighting and murder, and group response of ostracism, exile, or killing, i.e., "capital punishment." Intragroup anonymous violence is a void category for nomadic foragers; everyone knows everyone else in the group.

We turn now to intergroup violence. The term "intergroup" is tricky, as fission-fusion practices mean forager group membership is so fluid strict boundaries are difficult to establish. Nonetheless, there is evidence of intergroup personal violence or vengeance. Individual, personalized acts of fighting or murder sometimes call for a group response of delegating close kin to perform an individualized vengeance targeting only the murderer (Boehm 2012b). Using Boehm's reconstruction of the forager economy of violence, then, vengeance is an antiwar process; it prevents escalation to anonymous intergroup violence. So, for Boehm, forager economies of violence are (intragroup) antistate and (intergroup) antiwar.

We could say that Boehm is upping the ante on Nietzsche's *Genealogy* (Nietzsche 1997): "Of course the herd of weaklings ganged up and killed the solitary strong ones! You say that like it's a bad thing, when in fact, it's the secret of human evolution!" Of course, Nietzsche is not *complaining* about social selection or about the development of conscience (that which interferes with free-riding or domination by warning about group retribution); he's not resentful that this has occurred; he's not saying what he does as a moral argument about what *should* have happened—"see what you lot have done? wouldn't it have been better if the herd had stayed in its place way back when?" So, Boehm is not really defeating Nietzsche, since Nietzsche himself would certainly expect the descendants of herd maneuvers to think this way—"of course lambs do not like lions! Why should they?"

As we mentioned above, there is a vigorous debate as to whether pre-state nomadic forager bands engage in warfare. We have dealt with controversies about the archaeological record and about the biological continuity or "deep roots" thesis above in chapter 2; here we turn to ethnography, which might allow a careful extrapolation to pre-state conditions.

The ethnography of contemporary foragers shows multiple antiwar mechanisms, including delegation of vengeance to kin, thus
heading off feud. Feud—as opposed to vengeance—would allow
targeting any member of the other group, but this requires a "logic
of social substitution" that not all forager societies have (per Kelly
2000). Feud would be on the way to anonymous intergroup violence or war. In feud, there is collective duty to avenge wrongs that
is directed at a group that holds collective responsibility for the
wrongs committed by its members. According to Kelly (2000), this
pattern holds only in "segmented" societies (those in which mar-
riages and other social ties are regulated across subgroup formations such as lineages); many nomadic forager bands are "unsegmented" and hence practice only personalized vengeance rather
than collective feud.

Sterelny (2014) notes that foragers have no territorial motiva-
tion to attack, as they do not invest much labor into the land and
have no interest in permanent occupation (though this point is
nuanced by Scott (2017), who notes that permanent settlement is
compatible with foraging when a multi–food web site can be found
in resource-rich wetlands, whereby foragers can access multiple
food webs by remaining in place and allowing the resources to
come to them rather than having to chase the resources). Sterelny
also notes a psychological implausibility that war provided a selection pressure for our evolved traits of intragroup cooperation,
which does not seem compatible with also selecting for people
able to easily access the berserker rage useful in intergroup war. It
would be, Sterelny claims, too difficult to partition such aggressive
taking into only war; it would be too difficult to suppress its in-
group expression. But such in-group expression is what triggers
anti-alpha capital punishment, as we saw in chapter 2.

Kelly (2005) sketches a geo-eco-techno-social multiplicity that
results in a period of "intrinsic defensive advantage." The geographical aspect is that defenders know their territory and can
hold ambush positions. The ecological aspect is that low population density meant defenders can flee if needed. The technological

aspect is that single kill–capacity thrown weapons allow inflicting damage from afar on invaders with low risk to defenders. The social aspect is that invading parties would be nonspecialists while defenders would have throwing skills developed in hunting. Kelly concludes that, faced with such a period of defensive advantage, foragers developed positive, peace-seeking, intergroup mechanisms (diplomacy, feasts, contests).

With a universal-war anthropological perspective, you assume hostility is the default setting for intergroup relations, and war, prior to being territorially motivated, aims at women capture qua acquisition of reproductive resources. But this is not the only possible materialist position, as peace-seeking mechanisms are just as materialist as war. In fact, per Kelly (2005), they allow more efficient resource exploitation: the two sides are not afraid to exploit to the border of their territories, as they would be if border raids were frequent. For Kelly (2005), then, it's a shift to state military specialization that allows strikes at the home camp that shifts the balance and allows state territorial acquisition and enslavement warfare, as we will see in more detail in chapter 4.

### Sedentary Horticulturalists

Sedentary horticulturalists (also called the "autonomous village" social form) have chiefs; they do not command, though they do have perks and must show their prowess in warfare. The Yanomami people of South America are among the most well-studied of this kind of society (Clastres 1989; Chagnon 1988 Ferguson 1995).

Although one can criticize Clastres (and Deleuze and Guattari for taking on this point) for overgeneralizing from sedentary horticulturists to talk of "primitive society" that includes nomadic foragers (and thus overlooking crucial differences in their respective economies of violence), his discussion in "Society against the State" (the main essay of Clastres 1989) of "subsistence economy" and "imperial state slavery" is important and deserves some time here. (I'll maintain his use of the term "primitive," though of course his own concept of "non-state society" would be more acceptable today, as it eliminates the lingering evolutionism of the term "primitive.")

Clastres (1989) decries the political focus and ethnocentric bias of early accounts. As first-contact narratives are written by people of a state society, to them, a society without the state must be incomplete, lacking that which they should have, a king. The nineteenth-century "social evolutionists" see nonstate societies as a preliminary step in a progressive history, so that existing nomad foragers were "living fossils," a "window onto the past." For Clastres, the economic and technical focus of the anthropologists of his time is hardly better; for them, nonstate societies have only a "subsistence economy." Having no surplus implies incapacity to produce surplus, due to their inferior technology.

So Clastres sees two European prejudices in first-contact narratives, nineteenth-century evolutionists, and modern economic anthropology: politics must be the state and economics must be "work." For Clastres, the reality of primitive "technology" might not be "Cartesian" mastery of nature, but it does master their environment relative to their needs or they would have died or left. We always see a coevolving multiplicity: technology, social relations, and environment are interdependent processes with "intensive" relations (Clastres 1989, 192). Hence, to repeat a very widely held contemporary anthropological position, today's nomadic foragers are not "living fossils"; they are adapting to their (state-surrounded) eco-social environment.

So, what really is a "subsistence economy"? For Clastres, it is a European prejudice to say that subsistence is a constant scramble at edge of starvation, dissolution, or war with others (Clastres 1994, 105–18; see also Sahlins 1972; Widerquist and McCall 2017 summarize recent research that nuances Sahlins's often overly enthusiastic account). According to the "subsistence economy" prejudices, such a society does all it can just to let its members get a minimum survival. Yet, Clastres notes, we also see in first-contact narratives complaints about the "laziness" of natives:

they do what they need and then lounge about. So, it is an odd kind of edge-of-starvation "subsistence" if natives were healthy and had plenty of leisure.

For Clastres, "primitives" thus have all the time they would need to develop surplus if they so desired. They do not work for a surplus because they are not forced to externally. They refuse to produce a useless excess: they produce for their needs. In fact, they do produce a surplus that is then consumed in festivals when neighbors are invited. So, primitives refuse "work"; they have leisure and affluence (again, Sahlins 1972 and Widerquist and McCall 2017 should be consulted).

Among the reasons for Clastres's popularity, it seems to me, is his graphic description of initiation rites; for our purposes, these are crucial parts of the antistate mechanisms preserving the political positivity of "primitives" (Clastres 1989, 177–88). In being initiated, you are being obligated to distribute production in a way that prevents hoarding of personal property, and requires extravagant consumption. Initiation rites have an ambiguous position in an "economy of violence." Even though they can be "torturous," they are "voluntary" or better, key elements in social desiring-production. You are constituted by your desire to distribute to others and consume what they give you. So, for Clastres, initiation rites inscribe the "Anti-One" group law; they are hence antistate mechanisms (Clastres 1994, 93–104). In *Anti-Oedipus,* Deleuze and Guattari see initiation rites as antiexchange rites. They produce "mobile blocs of debt," and hence are antistate. Initiation ensures saturation of the social field with always-unequal relations and provokes "anti-production" that prevents stock (Deleuze and Guattari 1977, 184–92).

At this point we should pause to note that the use of "debt" by Deleuze and Guattari to indicate social obligations must be distinguished from the Nietzschean torture of "debtors." The use of "debt" by Nietzsche (1997) and by extension Deleuze and Guattari (1977) is criticized by David Graeber (2012) as projecting an individualism and a money economy onto pre-state society. Obligations in pre-state society are not oriented to restoration of precontract individuality as are "debts."

Now, sedentary horticultural chiefdoms are nonstate, but they do practice war. In fact, Clastres thought their form of warfare was an antistate process. Chiefs would have to continually prove their valor in war (Clastres 1994, 185), but precisely the high mortality rate would prevent their consolidation of power, enabling command relations rather than persuasion, and preventing nepotism. Political positivity of nonstate societies for Clastres resides in the way the locus of political power is the tribe itself, which holds "absolute and complete power over all the elements of which it is composed" (Clastres 1989, 207–12).

In Clastres's analyses, the clue to the political positivity of sedentary horticulturalists as nonstate societies is that the chief is not a king. Despite his prestige, the chief has no authority, no power, no coercion, no command. The locus of political power of the tribe is the tribe itself, not the chief, who serves the tribe. The function of the chief, per Clastres, is to resolve conflicts via his prestige used in oratory. Within the group, chiefs would persuade people in conflict to calm down, to emulate harmonious ancestors. Sometimes the chief will "play the chief" because he has no other choice. Due to his technical competence as war leader, he has a "minimum of authority." But he cannot convert (war-derived) prestige into (civil political) power. If the desire of the chief for war prestige matches that of (young men) in tribe, then all is well. But an overweening desire by the chief risks inverting his political relation to tribe as its servant. So, such hyperbolic desire might have been an origin of the state for Clastres. But this inverted political relation through excessive war desire never works. Because sometimes the society wants peace, and then the chief has to fight alone. He is thus "condemned to death in advance." Clastres's conclusion is that primitive society does not permit replacement of the chief's desire for prestige by a will-to-power that would institute a state-form of command in kingship (Clastres 1989, 189–218).

# 4. Origins of the State: James C. Scott, Statification, and *Marronage*

> Civilizational discourses never entertain the possibility of people voluntarily going over to the barbarians, hence such statuses are stigmatized and ethnicized.
>
> —JAMES C. SCOTT, *The Art of Not Being Governed*

IN THIS CHAPTER I put James C. Scott's works, in particular *The Art of Not Being Governed* (2009) and *Against the Grain* (2017), in conjunction with Deleuze and Guattari's notions of the economy of violence of statification processes. Although there is only a single citation to Deleuze and Guattari in these works (2009, 29), on what we below call the "mutual constitution" of state and nonstate processes), nonetheless we can identify four points of commonality; I will also note places where Scott makes important contributions independent of this framework.

First, they share an anti-evolutionist position, such that states are not the telos of a progressive development of social forms but a contested social form whose imposition and retention depends on local and contingent conditions. Second, they agree that statification and *marronage,* or flight from the state, are coexisting and mutually constitutive processes. That is, as soon as there were states, people ran for the hills, but states are themselves dependent on their surrounding hill people, who only become "nonstate" by the state's attempt to capture and hold them. Third, they agree that the statification processes of territorial control and appropriation of surplus are mutually constituting, such that the success of states depends on the full functionality of multiple processes, creating the sense that the fully formed state must arrive all at once as "Urstaat." And fourth, they agree on the need to conceptually separate the primary or originary violence of statification as capture and enslavement of nonstate peoples, and the ordinary, everyday, or secondary violence of tax collection and labor coercion, which repeat and reinforce the originary violence by which tax and labor become obligations.

## Scott's Anti-Evolutionist Method

Scott's stated aim in *The Art of Not Being Governed* is to criticize social evolutionist theories in which statification fits a progress narrative. Rather, for him, "state" and "non-state" processes are in "dialectical" (Scott 2009, 2) or "symbiotic" (2009, 26), that is, mutually constituting relations. Although Scott doesn't use Deleuze and Guattari's specialized vocabulary, his theses on mutual constitution and anti-evolutionism means he shares with them the sense that statification is only one of several socializing "abstract machines" or "diagrams," whose success or failure at being actualized in any one time and place depends on local and contingent conditions.

In the remainder of this section, I will rearrange the order of presentation in the Preface to *Art* to emphasize those of Scott's methodological principles that illustrate these points. In articulating each of his three main principles (anti–state centrism; anti-progressivism; antideterminism) there is a dialectic of capture and escape that is a theoretical mirror of the historical processes being examined: first, a critical interpretation of how state thought has captured our views of nonstate people and then a positive project of examining the practices of self-governing peoples.

Scott's anti–state centrism has two moves. First, there is a critical interpretation of state denigration of the other, as in the epigraph to this chapter (2009, x–xi). Scott's positive project then is writing the history of nonstate peoples as the complement of state-centered history:

The huge literature on state-making, contemporary and historic, pays virtually no attention to its obverse: the history of deliberate and reactive statelessness. This is the history of those who got away, and state-making cannot be understood apart from it. This is also what makes this an anarchist history. (2009, x)

Next, let us consider Scott's antiprogressivism. Here we first see a critical interpretation of state-progress narratives. From a state perspective, "self-governing peoples" are "living ancestors," a glimpse of pre-agricultural, precivilized life. Here Scott alludes to a politics of anthropology, a way that progressivism or evolutionism is put to work, legitimating incorporation of nonstate peoples to allow them access to modernity. Scott argues, on the contrary, "hill people are best understood as runaway, fugitive, maroon communities who have, over the course of two millennia, been fleeing the oppression of state-making projects in the valleys—slavery, conscription, taxes, corvée labor, epidemics, and warfare" (2009, ix; see also Roberts 2015).

This critical setup leads to his positive project of describing "primitivism" as antistate strategy.

The argument reverses much received wisdom about "primitivism" generally. Pastoralism, foraging, shifting cultivation, and segmentary lineage systems are often a "secondary adaptation," a kind of "self-barbarization" adopted by peoples whose location, subsistence, and social structure are adapted to state evasion. For those living in the shadow of states, such evasion is also perfectly compatible with derivative, imitative, and parasitic state forms in the hills. (2009, x)

Finally, Scott pursues a double aspect antideterminism analysis. First, he provides a critical interpretation of ecological and cultural determinism, or, simply stated, he puts the politics into "political economy":

Usually, forms of subsistence and kinship are taken as given, as ecologically and culturally determined. By analyzing various forms of cultivation, particular crops, certain social structures, and physical mobility patterns for their escape value, I treat such givens as political choices. (2009, xi)

He complements that with his positive project of describing anti-state practices:

> physical dispersion in rugged terrain, their mobility, their cropping practices, their kinship structures, their pliable ethnic identities, and their devotion to prophetic, millenarian leaders all serve to avoid incorporation into states and to prevent states from springing up among them. (2009, x)

## Scott's Multiplicity

Alongside the mutual constitution and anti-evolutionist theses examined above, another element shared by Scott with Deleuze and Guattari is the way Scott describes statification and *marronage* as a multiplicity or set of interlinking processes that describes qualitative changes when thresholds in the relations of those processes are reached.

The elements of Scott's multiplicity include topographical-transport-technological, political-economic, political-organizational, administrative, and violence elements. Although Scott does allow that "stateness" could be seen on an "institutional continuum" (2017, 23), nonetheless there is a "strong" sense of the term in which we see a necessary interlocking of statification processes ("territoriality and a specialized state apparatus: walls, tax collection, officials" [2017, 118]) centered on "control and appropriation" (2017, 116). Such a strong sense of stateness reminds one of Deleuze and Guattari's notion of the state as "apparatus of capture" and their concomitant "Urstaat" thesis. Only the state brings mono-crop grain agriculture and coerced appropriation by a predatory stratum together; none of the temporally preceding social forms, even if they have some elements that are later taken up into the state, can be said to be early developmental forms of the state (2017, 117). The Urstaat thesis, then, comes down to a way of describing the qualitative leap into the state, which is not simply a large chiefdom or a hierarchical, nepotistic band, but its own form, achieved together or not at all (Sibertin-Blanc 2016; Smith 2018).

Let us begin with the topographical-transport-technological processes, or what Scott calls the "friction of terrain" (2009, 43 *et passim*; 2017, 116–49). Spaces open to early statification are valleys and rivers allowing for military enforcement, administrative "visibility," and economic integration. These are all limited by cost per unit weight across distance, which, with ancient technologies, are much easier by water, as land transport by human and animal power is constrained by its need for fuel, which it also had to carry with it. Nonstate spaces in *Art* are mostly hills and mountains, but include any region where state military reach is hampered, such as jungles, deserts, marshes, and so on (2009, 13). These transport processes intersect the production aspect of the region's political economy. States are able to appropriate river valley grain agriculture due to its "legibility." Grain is taxable or able to be directly appropriated, and the grain-growing population can be conscripted into military service or into corvée labor for infrastructure or monuments. Scott also describes the use of enslavement by the capture of hill people by raiding or by debt bondage, as well as sharecropping (2017, 150–82).

Economic practices that are tolerated or encouraged by states include independent urban artisanal production, temple and palace luxury goods (also by trade or gift), and the production of goods for trade with hill peoples, such as fish and other foods unavailable in the hills and manufactured goods (e.g., metal tools and weapons). When it comes to nonstate production, we see auto-consumed food and trade. Food production and consumption comes from swidden agriculture or horticulture, from nomadic steppe pastoralism, and from nomadic foraging. Exchange with states by hill people takes the form of sale, barter, debt payment, tribute (2009, 106).

Finally, Scott treats ethnic, kinship, and linguistic structures. State systems need ease of incorporation in order to concentrate populations, even if we see use of ethnicity for stratification. When incorporating nonstate peoples, states make membership in multiple kinship systems into fixed tribal identities in a process of "ethnogenesis" (2009, 238–82; 257–59). But what the state calls "ethnicity" is to the hill peoples a fluid strategy allowing them to claim different identities, depending who was asking. Tribal forms are often state creations for administration, though they can become a self-identity for political purposes. Nonstate kinship allows an ease of incorporation of immigrants, captives, in-marrying, as well as an ease of creating fictitious lineages to legitimate new aristocratic attempts. And finally, hill peoples tend to multilingualism (2009, 239; 269).

## The Economy of Violence of Statification

When it comes to political organization, Scott notes that state-building projects require—and aim at, in mutual presupposition—concentrated manpower, central command, military specialization, taxes, and corvée labor. As we sketched in chapter 3, this mutual presupposition is what Deleuze and Guattari call the "pre-accomplishment" of the violence of statification; in this chapter, we see how it undergirds the anti-evolutionist "Urstaat" thesis, the way in which state success depends on all its components working together, so that is seems to arrive in history all at once (Deleuze and Guattari 1977, 217–22; 1987, 427; see also Sibertin-Blanc 2016 and Smith 2018). Let us consider now some of the details we can find in putting Scott's account in contact with Deleuze and Guattari's framework.

In *State and Politics,* Guillaume Sibertin-Blanc (2016) has precisely demonstrated the temporal and structural complication of Deleuze and Guattari's discussion of early statification (see also Smith 2018). Sibertin-Blanc focuses on the relation between, on the one hand, the actual history of nonstate and state societies, and, on the other hand, the postulated mechanisms by which nonstate societies evade or "conjure" the virtual potential of the state that is always immanent to their functions. Overall then, Sibertin-Blanc investigates what Deleuze and Guattari have to say about the relation of "concrete assemblages" (this or that band, village, or state) and "abstract machines" (the diagrams of "primitive society" and "the state").

The real question for Deleuze and Guattari (and Clastres, with whom they are in dialogue) is the emergence of statification as that which destroys nonstate societies. For them, it is impossible to conceive an internal mutation of the society leading the way, as primitives would have to desire to change, but following the notion of desiring-production sketched in *Anti-Oedipus,* their whole way of life produces a different form of desire. For Deleuze and Guattari, "economics" as production, distribution, and consumption is not divorced from social relations in primitive society. Nonstate peoples do not have jobs that are independent of family relations; rather, what one produces, distributes, and consumes is determined by your family relations. Since "desire" for Deleuze and Guattari is not about lack but about flows and breaks, then one desires that flows be produced and channeled in a particular pattern of "desiring-production"; in this case, those flows are coded by family relations (and later "overcoded" by the state's apparatus of capture.)

Deleuze and Guattari follow Clastres in claiming there must be an external political force that imposes social, political, and economic transformation. Thus, they do not see the state as a mere instrument of a preexisting ruling and owning class. If there were a prior difference in force allowing an exploitative class, the logic goes, why bother constructing a state to wield force that already exists? Similarly, if the state protects preexisting private property, how does that arise in primitive society dedicated to refusing private property? Sibertin-Blanc puts this in terms of a commentary on Wittfogel (1957): the state is not the instrument of preexisting dominant class; it is itself the direct organization of society enabling surplus production that it then immediately appropriates (Sibertin-Blanc 2016). In other words, the primary violence of statification is that which produces the dominant and subordinate classes.

This is where Sibertin-Blanc lets us see what Deleuze and Guattari are doing with their notion of the "Urstaat" and the "auto-presupposition" of the state: the state needs a surplus to feed its specialists but it needs specialists to produce its surplus. Further, they replace Clastres's mysterious "presentiment" of the state by the primitives with an analysis of the mechanisms of "anticipation" and "conjuration" in which the distinction between limit and threshold allows them to analyze always-existing tendencies and the virtual thresholds that would require changing the social machine (Deleuze and Guattari 1987, 438).

For Sibertin-Blanc, there's always an undecidability in the notion of Urstaat as a theory of state form; Deleuze and Guattari's work is both a materialist history of an apparatus of power (a rewriting of, e.g., Engels's *Origin of the Family, Private Property, and the State*) and an analysis of historical desire, collective subjectivation, and group fantasy (a rewriting of, e.g., Freud's *Totem and Taboo*) (Sibertin-Blanc 2016). In the realm of desiring-production, the question is how to reorient desiring-production from primitive immanent horizontalism (that is, saturation of the social field by always-unequal obligations ["mobile blocs of debt"]) to a transcendent hierarchical centralization with an infinite debt owed to the emperor. For Sibertin-Blanc, this is the problem of desire Clastres never solved; he could show how the primitive machine wards off the state by the production of desire for war prestige in the chiefs, as well as desire for equality and free time by everyone, but could never show how it became desire for the state. That was always a mystery to Clastres (Sibertin-Blanc 2016).

To work around Clastres's dilemma, Sibertin-Blanc proposes that Deleuze and Guattari deconstruct the problem of the historical origin of the state. It is impossible to identify the state with its material apparatuses. First, you have to account for statification by historical materialist means; but, second, evolutionist accounts face aporias that problematize the self-presupposition and self-production of the state. Simply put, you need surplus to feed military and administrative specialists but you need military and administrative specialists to enslave and exploit (turn primitives into peasants who owe debts to emperor). Thus, Sibertin-

Blanc and Clastres agree that "economic anthropology" needs to self-destruct and become political economy. You cannot "objectively" cross-compare the "production" and "surplus" of nonstate and state societies. You can only compare production levels when "work" is instituted. But then you have to talk statification as capture and enslavement.

Before we move to Scott's deep history of the first states, let us here provide a brief discussion of Scott's work on the abstract forms of statification processes, where we see Deleuze and Guattari's themes in action. Population concentration is needed for agriculture and for the military to squeeze producers, and to hold geographically important positions to collect tolls on trade (Scott 2009, 64; 2017, 150–82). Control of such populations requires central command authority with radiating subordinates in charge of military specialization aiming at enforcement of payment for taxes in the form of land rents based on "legible" agricultural productivity and in the form of tolls and other taxes on commercial transactions. Finally, centralized administration and enforcement is needed for corvée labor. All those state-building practices, along with famines and epidemics, increase the incentive for flight from states to nonstate "shatter zones" where we find various nonstate political forms, such as egalitarian bands, chiefdoms, and temporary alliances (2009, 24, 326).

Scott's treatment of the violence of statification (2017, 150–82) thus provides a point of contact with Deleuze and Guattari. Scott implicitly accepts the distinction between the "primary violence" of statification warfare aiming at territorial incorporation and at population enslavement and resettlement, from the "secondary violence" of terror aimed at tax collection and at the enforcement of conscription and corvée labor. Initial and ongoing statification violence finds its counterparts among nonstate peoples in fighting against state agents, internal state-preventing violence, and predation on state economies in targeting trade routes for robbery or extortion of tolls, in raids that steal from the produce of valley agricultural producers, and also slave capture, in which valley population is itself the target, a commodity to be sold to competing states (Scott 2017, 219–56).

## Scott's Deep History of the First States

Shifting now to Scott's treatment of the actual historical record, we will see many of the elements discussed in Sibertin-Blanc's reading of Deleuze and Guattari in Scott's *Against the Grain* (2017). Scott's primary aim is to overturn the usual progress narrative in which states are the telos of a development in social forms. His themes are the following: (1) the independence, and precedence, of sedentism relative to statification; (2) domestication, including that of humans, via the disciplined reduction in dimensionality of biosocial life; (3) the self-induced fragility of the "domus," the assemblage of sedentary humans and their surrounding domesticated flora and fauna; (4) statification as the capture of the domus making it the niche-construction of elites; (5) the fragility of early states, prompting escape of domesticated populations; and (6) the "Golden Age of barbarians," the way in which states provided new predation opportunities for the nonstate peoples they create in statification. Each of these themes reinforce the theses of anti-evolutionism, mutual constitution of state and nonstate processes, the necessary interlocking of statification processes, and the economy of violence of statification that Scott shares with Deleuze and Guattari.

Scott begins by recalling that most years of *H. sapiens* life was in nomadic, acephalic, forager bands, and that stratified, taxed, walled-in agricultural states only appear about five thousand years ago (thus 3000 BCE). These earliest states, however, appear four thousand years after crop domestication and sedentism. The state is thus not an outgrowth of a smooth development of economic practices; rather it is a contingent imposition of command and of reduced dimensionality on preexisting diversified food production practices allowing appropriation of surplus from mono-grain-crop agriculture to various strata of nonprimary producers (2017, 21–24, 116–18).

Scott hammers away at the fact that sedentism is not the result of fixed agriculture, for sedentism first shows up thousands of years earlier in ecologically rich and varied wetlands (2017, 10, 68–92). There is another discordance between sedentism and agriculture, as there were also people who planted crops and then dispersed until returning for harvest. Also, harvest tools preceded planting, so humans were living on harvested wild plants well before planting them in agriculture. Thus, we had a long period of low-level plant food provisioning that was not fully wild, yet not fully domesticated either. We can therefore see a long history of various domestications qua control of reproduction of plants, animals, and humans (most intensely but not exclusively in captured slave women (2017, 37–67). States thus appear long after fixed-field agriculture, and these early states were not always or even especially attractive, contra the logic of the social contract tradition; they had to capture and hold population, but that exposes them to epidemics, so they were fragile (2017, 25–30, 150–82). Furthermore, states create new predation opportunities for "barbarians," who were better off than rural peasants and certainly slaves (2017, 219–56).

Although I am interested in the overlap of Scott and Deleuze and Guattari, I also want to note the independence of Scott's thought. In one of his most interesting long-view perspectives, Scott looks at human social organization as dipping into a set of domestication practices producing control of the physical (and psychological, when possible) reproduction of fire, plants, animals, slaves, subjects, and women. These are brought together in the "domus" or "Neolithic resettlement camp," an assemblage or concatenation of multiple species and environmental features—landscape changes, animal pens, houses, butcher shops, blacksmiths, marketplaces, and so on—that are put together in varying proportions. The domus represents an attempt at a multidimensional, long-term inherited niche construction (2017, 70).

So, given the domus as the site of multispecies domestication, Scott asks in one of his probing questions, can we see a domestication of humans over time (2017, 83–92)? Scott's work here is compatible with the Human Self-Domestication hypothesis we discussed in chapter 2, which looks at top-down anger control and bottom-up reduction in reactivity as processes allowing pre-state egalitarian forager band life (Hare 2017; Gonzalez-Cabrera 2017). Scott's claims imply what would be an acceleration of that process with the domus assemblage, with one of his points being the bimodal fossil record with a small group resembling pre-state foragers and a larger group (presumably of "domesticated" workers) with nutritional and growth problems (2017, 84, 107–9). It should be noted that Scott does not discuss the possibility of biocultural evolution in the Developmental Systems Theory mode (Oyama, Griffiths, and Gray 2001). However, even if you do not accept the full concept of inherited epigenetic changes, as long as you have roughly convergent child-rearing practices you can produce more docility or aggression depending on the class one is born into. In practical terms, a social system can make a high percentage of boys into soldiers or warriors or peasants by their upbringing.

Over time, Scott says, we can see a vast reduction in the dimensionality of life via increasing "discipline." Foragers have to be acquainted with the behavior and rhythms of many, many species and food webs as they intersect the seasonal rhythms and local weather of their area. Farming, then, is the intentional reduction of those dimensions to much fewer: a cereal crop, plus some domesticated animals. (Domesticating animals involves reduction of dimensions, for domestication of food animals is making them helpless prey by working ahead of time to breed docility and confine space for the animals to turn what was difficult hunting into easy slaughter.) Hence, there is a big reduction in rhythms to a fairly simple one of plowing, planting, tending, and harvesting, so that in a sense we become dependent on our creations, the domesticates. The reduced dimensions of yeoman farming can be further routinized or "deskilled" in labor practices, such that the assembly line—whether in an industrial factory or in a large routinized slave plantation—is thus a further reduction in dimensions (2017, 87–92).

A final dimension of domestication and discipline comes from control of female reproduction in response to the fragility of the domus. The domus is fragile due to the density-dependent diseases that the domus itself allows to flourish by bringing together multiple species of plants and animals, which thus bring together the insects, pests, vermin, and microorganisms they carry with them. So, a lot of farming work is protecting crops from these dangers that farming itself produces. The domus is also fragile because of a reduction in produced food sources, a reduction that requires constant inputs from the "nature" it tries to keep outside. But the domus allows for a huge spike in reproduction that outweighs the increased death costs. If we compare forager population control, we see delayed weaning, abortion, infanticide, high-exercise lives with low body fat and high-protein diets delay menarche and can make menstruation irregular. For foragers, a child is a mouth to feed for many years, but for farmers, a child is a labor source. So, female reproduction becomes an important economic factor to be disciplined in the domus (2017, 111–14).

Returning to the overlap of Scott with Deleuze and Guattari, we see that statification is in Scott's terms the "targeting" of the domus assemblage—agriculture, domestic animals, towns, specialized work—for the "niche-construction" of elites (Scott 2017, 122). The domus is captured so that elites can appropriate the surplus that is produced; you could even say they are parasites. You can have agriculture, sedentism, and towns without states, but you cannot have states without monoculture of grains. That is because, for Scott, one of the main characteristics of states is taxation, and nongrain food production is much harder to effectively tax (117–18).

Scott does pose the temporal question of how the state got off the ground, giving some credence to the thought that drought might have packed people together and diminished resource diversity (120–22). But such environmental factors would only provide a contingently arriving necessary condition. Overall, Scott's analyses fit Deleuze and Guattari's Urstaat thesis of the necessity of assembling state forms all at once in a mutually constitutive, functioning unit: taxation, including the special apparatus of collectors, assessors, accountants; work gangs for agriculture or monumental architecture; scribes and their recordkeeping apparatus; military specialists; standardized weights and measures. Scott calls this the harnessing of the "grain and manpower module as a basis of control and appropriation" (116).

As we have seen, the domus was already insecure, so adding state parasitism on top of it only increased the strain through two main elements of the statification economy of violence: first, taxation scooping into the surplus and hence pushing farmers to the edge of survival, and second, frequent warfare, which further exposed farming surplus to further appropriation either through heightened war taxation or plunder by invading armies. Scott implies that taxation is a sort of rationalized, regularized plunder by rulers of a domesticated population, analogous to the replacement of hunting by slaughter of domesticated animals (146).

To secure states against this fragility we find an important aspect of the economy of violence. Preventing flight via territorial control was essential to early states; Scott asks us to compare the Spanish *reducciones* or settlement camps in the New World. Such control is necessary in order for elites to appropriate surplus, which is otherwise produced and consumed by foragers in their commons-based system. Peasants, by contrast, have to be coerced; this can be directly by enslavement, corvée labor, and debt bondage, or later by simple control of land with a dense population so that independent access to the land is impossible. Thus, another prime requirement is stopping flight, or regular war to replace lost population by enslavement, by slave purchase from "barbarians," or forced resettlement of populations brought from a conquered territory elsewhere (151–53).

As we have mentioned, some of Scott's most interesting passages do not have a direct corollary in Deleuze and Guattari, thus indicating Scott's importance as an independent thinker. Another example of this is Scott's work on slavery as "human resources" strategy (2017, 167–70). Scott is careful to note that states did not invent slavery, which existed in chiefdoms, but it did ramp it up significantly. Prisoners of war were a source of slaves; wars were as much or more slave raids than territorial enhancement, as population replacement on the land already under control was as important as expanding territory, which just increases the need for population control (154–59).

In his analysis of enslavement in the economy of violence of early statification, Scott begins by noting that slave capture means a state can acquire the productive years of a human, with the cost of raising them—and developing their skills—borne by other regimes. Enslavement with transport from a homeland to foreign soil is also deracination and atomization, so states can pit individual slaves against an entire social assemblage of violence aimed at their control. The desirable productivity of adult male slaves had to be balanced against the possibility of revolt, which increases if when slaves have ethnic ties, a common language, and a memory of freedom. Hence there is often a preference for women and children as slave captives, both for docility and to provide reproduction of the slave population, or, with manumission and assimilation, a means of replenishing the local work force. Finally, Scott shows how slavery helps social stratification, both by using slaves as rewards to elites and by sparing the local workers from the worst exploitation and thus heading off their insurrection (167–70).

Scott's descriptions allow us to see both structural and overt elements of the economy of violence of statification. The "structural violence" of early states comes from their very high death rates through disease and malnutrition (191–95). There is of course also overt violence in what Scott calls "politicide," or failure of actual states from mismanagement of statification processes. Grain-population assemblage requires manpower to produce but also to defend territory and in aggressive wars to replace population, but this only puts more pressure on the remaining primary producers and hence increases their desire to flee, which in turn requires more surveillance by nonproducers, and so on (203).

Finally, in a clear explication of the "mutual constitution thesis" of state and nonstate peoples, Scott analyzes the economy of violence of state and nonstate processes in what he calls the "Golden Age of Barbarians." Captive state populations increase the quality of barbarian prey targets. We can contrast this quick, acute raiding with the rationalized raiding that is state taxation (223, 238). More importantly, however, states were trading partners for barbarians. Raw material (e.g., timber), exotic goods (spices), as well as cattle and slaves were traded for textiles, jewelry, grain, pottery, and so on (222–23, 237).

Barbarian geography relies on the "friction of terrain," as Scott says in *Art of Not Being Governed.* State armies were based on infantry and cavalry, so getting into forests and hills frustrated state control attempts. Borders between state and "barbarian" spaces were two-way membranes, not one-way as a social contract narrative would have it. As a result, we see the following interlocking and mutually constituting processes: state and nonstate populations could shift modes of production from farming and herding mixes to foraging and back again, but as state formation produced refugees, then-established states always had flight issues (as well as high mortality), such that slave raids and forced resettlement of nonstate peoples were necessary (228–31).

In keeping with the anti-evolution thesis, many "barbarians" were ex–state subjects heading back to foraging or "secondary primitivism," as Scott notes in referring to Clastres. Recalling his analyses in *Art,* here in *Against the Grain* Scott also names upland zones as "shatter zones" of population and cultural mixing. From these scatter zones, domesticated farmers were tempting targets, but raiding had to be kept in check to avoid resource depletion, so smart barbarians shifted to tribute qua protection racket, thus mimicking the state (232, 240–43).

Turning to the political-organization aspect of the mutual-constitution thesis, Scott has states and barbarians as symbionts or "dark twins" that sometimes produced a sort of shared sovereignty (or sharing of appropriated surplus), but their relation could break down (249–50). So, barbarians and states are competing for ability to extract surplus from captive primary production populations (243). Barbarian control of trade routes enabled them to trade with states and also to extort "taxation" of state traders via "tolls" to allow passage, and piracy as predation on state trading. Barbarians did not always flee or repel the state; sometime they conquered it and became the new ruling class, and at other times they became mercenaries of state armies (250–51). While the "Golden Age" of barbarians lasted a long time, enslavement of other barbarians and sale of military service ultimately tipped the scales in favor of states, which now dominate the globe to a much greater extent than ever before (255–56).

As a transition to our final chapter, let us note that, although Scott doesn't explore it in *Against the Grain,* you can follow his analysis of contemporary state domination in *Seeing Like a State* and *The Art of Not Being Governed*: despite failures of central planning, more modest administration can keep internal population management going very nicely in the core—going off the grid or creating police no-go zones in slums notwithstanding. In the periphery, brutality with automatic weapons, helicopters, and GPS can keep peasantry in line and keep nonstate people confined to margins and ineffective in resisting resource extraction when desired. This is not to say that sheer force is confined to the periphery; what we see in so-called no-go zones is a sort of "shared sovereignty" between nonstate actors—in Scott's terms, "barbarian" gangs—and state police forces, who arrive in force when they want to and shoot first and ask questions later.

With these last points, we come to the topic of chapter 5: the reproduction of the state form and the role of ideology and force therein.

# 5. Fractures of the State: Deleuze and Guattari on Ideology

> Granted, then, that the supreme mystery of despotism, its prop
> and stay, is to keep men in a state of deception, and with the
> specious title of religion to cloak the fear by which they must
> be held in check, so that they will fight for their servitude as
> if for their salvation, and count it no shame, but the highest
> honor, to spend their blood and their lives for the glorification
> of one man.
>
> —SPINOZA, *Tractatus Theologico-Politicus*

DELEUZE AND GUATTARI loved to provoke their readers, and "ideology is an execrable concept"—found in both *Anti-Oedipus* and
*A Thousand Plateaus*—is one of their best provocations. Not too
many folks, surprisingly, have taken the bait, and when they do, it
is either explication or denunciation. I would like here to have a
look at what they say about ideology in order to see what we can
do with it, what kind of machine we can construct with it.

This chapter has four sections. First, I show how ideology is
supposed to explain social reproduction, the production and reproduction of "bodies politic." Second, I explain how Deleuze
and Guattari think ideology is composed of beliefs, and why such
a conception cannot explain a particular case of bodies politic,
fascism, because it cannot handle subpersonal body-political
affective-cognitive patterning or "desire." Third, I explain
Deleuze and Guattari's nonideological notion of microfascism as
that form of desire for control and "Power" that spreads throughout a society, enabling a macrofascist state. Fourth, I construct a

notion of "affective ideology" that can better account for social reproduction than the "mere belief" notion that Deleuze and Guattari criticize.

## What Is Ideology Supposed to Explain?

Ideology is supposed to explain noncoerced social reproduction, that is, the production and reproduction of "bodies politic." It is very often limited to cognitive errors that distort the perception of social reality in unequal societies by masking exploitation, but I would like to expand it in two directions: (1) to cover shared ways of life in equal societies, and (2) to include the affective as well as the cognitive.

"Ideology" has a psychological and a functional sense. Psychologically, ideology is the process that produces a rough coincidence of body political affective-cognitive patterns of an entire society. What is shared is an orientation to the world such that objects appear with characteristic affective tones: an enculturated person will not experience just "this action" but "this beautiful and graceful action that everyone should admire," or "this grotesque and shameful action that should be punished." Functionally, the sharing of affective-cognitive orientation we call "ideology" contributes to the stability and reproducibility of social patterns of thought and practice on daily, lifespan, and generational scales. (For discussion of shared intentionality and the cooperative motives that enable it, see Tomasello 2009 and 2016. For early cultural learning fulfilling the psychological sense of ideology—transmitting the basic concepts of a society, including those of technical procedures, see Sterelny 2012.)

This is not to deny the existence of puzzling experiences, which do not fit the preexisting concepts, or moral dilemmas, in which an action is susceptible of multiple and conflicting interpretations. Without wanting to produce a full phenomenological description of those cases, but simply to insist on the essential co-presence of affect and cognition in experience, note that there is a characteristic affective tone of puzzlement, or of being stuck, of being pulled in two (or indeed more) directions, or of hewing to and fro between commitments. And that we often experience a felt sense of relief in having made a decision, or foreboding at the outcome of our decision, or a sense of resignation to our fate, or a sense of commitment to the type of person we are making of ourselves by this decision, and so on and so forth.

Ideological social reproduction is noncoercive, but no one thinks social reproduction happens by shared affective-cognitive patterns alone; all societies have practices of physical force that can, at least in theory and when properly applied, punish or eliminate those prone to system-damaging behavior such as free-riding or bullying. Call that coercive social pattern "reproduction."

So, we want to be able to see the relation of the psychological and functional senses of ideology to each other and the relation of that pair to coercive reproduction.

While no one thinks shared ideology alone is enough to ensure social reproduction, some hold that contemporary societies have rendered the functional sense of ideology otiose via sophisticated forms of coercive reproduction and their attendant collective action problems (Rosen 1996). As I will explain, I do not share that position; I think ideological buy-in on the part of a critical portion of the enforcers of coercive reproduction is necessary, but only with a notion of ideology expanded to include the affective.

In small egalitarian societies, sharing affective-cognitive patterns via enculturation supports shared productive and reproductive labor via shared intentionality; hence we see the psychological and functional senses of ideology as noncoercive social reproduction. Furthermore, as we have seen above, due to small size and mostly transparent shared production, the identification of the few cases of free-riders and bullies allows coercive social reproduction via punishment via ridicule, ostracism, exile, or execution (Boehm 2012b; Sterelny 2016).

In societies with unequal distributions of goods beyond a certain threshold of inequality we see, alongside interest-concordant behavior, the appearance of interest-discordant behavior (assuming that the inequality in question is such that those on the short end are deprived of a level of goods necessary for their interests as human beings capable of flourishing, a notion we might flesh out by reference to the "capabilities" in Nussbaum 1993). Deleuze and Guattari call the puzzle of interest-discordant behavior "Reich's question": why are theft and strikes not the general, rather than the exceptional, response to poverty and exploitation? Allied to that is Spinoza's question: "why do men fight for their servitude as fiercely as for their freedom?"

In unequal societies, ideology entails the sharing, throughout the society, of affective-cognitive patterns proclaiming the system to be fair and thus for the elites to have been justly rewarded (psychological sense) so that this coincidence contributes to the reproduction of the system (functional sense). The ideology of meritocracy and elite superiority helps reproduce the system by epistemic and emotional processes. Elites do not see the injustice of the system and thereby feel justified in their success, thus protecting interest-concordant behavior from interference by guilt feelings should their benefits appear to have been unearned. For oppressed people who internalize their oppression—if such people exist—there is an epistemic effect of hiding the systematic sources of their social position, and an emotional effect of resistance-inhibiting "justified" inferiority feelings, thus protecting interest-discordant behavior from interference by feelings of righteous indignation ("system justification theory" as in Jost, Federico, and Napier 2009).

Coercive reproduction works by punishment producing expectations of the same for future deviations. We will focus on the role of ideology in enabling the internal discipline of the punishment forces deployed in coercive reproduction. Are police, army, and workplace personnel (from security guards to slave overseers) kept in place merely by practices of external rewards (raises, promotions, and esteem of their fellows for good behavior) and punishments (fines, demotions, dismissal, execution for deviation)?

That is, are there effective collective-action problems produced by coercive reproduction practices targeting them, the enforcers? Call that lateral coercive reproduction. Or does that system of lateral coercive reproduction itself require an ideological buy-in on the part of at least some portion of the enforcers for them to do their work of disciplining the others who produce the punishment practices contributing to—or wholly responsible for—large-scale social reproduction? And finally, does that notion of ideological buy-in on the part of (some portion of) the enforcers not have to include an affective dimension?

## Deleuze and Guattari: Ideology as Belief-Structure

In *Anti-Oedipus,* "ideology" is criticized because it focuses on the cognitive and neglects the affective-cognitive, or "desire," the direct libidinal investment of social structures.

> Reich is at his greatest as a thinker when he refuses to accept ignorance or illusion on the part of the masses as an explanation of fascism, and demands an explanation in terms of desire: no, the masses were not duped, under certain circumstances they desired fascism, and it is this perversion of mass desire we have to explain. (Deleuze and Guattari 1977, 29–30)

As Deleuze and Guattari see it, ideology critique seeks to correct the irrationality that masks a vision of what rational social production would and should look like. But for them that sort of being fooled as to social reality is not where the action is; what they say we need to explain are not cognitive errors but perverse desires. Hence, interest-contrary behavior is

> not a question of ideology. There is an unconscious libidinal investment of the social field, which coexists but does not necessarily coincide with preconscious investments, or with that which the preconscious investments "should be." That's why, when subjects—individuals or groups—go manifestly against their class interests, when they adhere to the interests and ideas of a class that their own objective situation should determine them to combat, it's not enough to say: they have been fooled, the masses have

been fooled. It's not an ideological problem of misrecognition and illusion, it's a problem of desire, *and desire is part of the infra-structure*. (1977, 104)

What's perverse about fascist desire is that it is desire desiring its own repression. Deleuze and Guattari distinguish psychic re-pression (*refoulement*) and social repression (*répression*). They always say Wilhelm Reich (1946) is correct about the priority of social over psychic repression, but Reich's problem is reinstalling a distinction between rational social production (e.g., government provision of infrastructure through political decisions arrived at after deliberation in a system of rationally justified social struc-tures) and irrational fantasies (we're being swamped by a flood of immigrants so we need a strong leader).

So even though Reich had insisted that the real question is un-der which sociopolitical conditions—and I would add bio-affective conditions—rates and intensities and waves of anxiety, fear, de-pression, rage passing through the population—did the masses come to desire fascism, he still pushes the old split between de-sire as irrational fantasy and production as rational reality, instead of seeing desiring-production. Thus, for Deleuze and Guattari, Reich's brand of psychoanalysis can only find in social desire what is negative and inhibited, not what is positively produced: "But, because [Reich] had not sufficiently formed the concept of desiring-production, he didn't succeed in determining how de-sire is inserted in the economic infrastructure, the insertion of the drives into social production" (118). Desiring-production is the di-rect libidinal investment in flow-breaks: foragers are happy when meat circulates, imperial subjects feel something as they see the palace of the emperor (negative investment is still investment), Christian subjects feel rapture as the icon circulates. Capitalist li-bidinal investment occurs through the double structure of money, as the same units are used for the "giant mutant flow" of generated credit, and in the paychecks of employees and the collection cups of beggars (229).

In *A Thousand Plateaus,* Reich is dropped but Deleuze and Guattari produce their own complex account of microfascism: "Only microfascism provides an answer to the global question: Why does desire desire its own repression, how can it desire its own repression?" (Deleuze and Guattari 1987, 215).

### Deleuze and Guattari on Microfascism

So, let us turn to Deleuze and Guattari on microfascism in *A Thousand Plateaus,* where it is seen as a "cancerous Body without Organs." (Hereafter, "BwO"; my analysis here is based on Protevi 2018, commenting on Deleuze and Guattari 1987, 149–66 and 208–31.) The "enemy" of the organs is not the BwO but the organism, a centralized, hierarchical patterning of the organs (which are flow-break machines). Deleuze and Guattari's notion of the organism can be articulated with Damasio's somatic marker theory of emotion in which a subject of emotional experience arises from a singular state of the body. An "organism" permits itself some connections while forbidding itself others. The "neurobiologico-desiring machines" (Deleuze and Guattari 1977, 63) form an "organism" when their patterns produce a body that serves its social machine.

The "cancerous" Body without Organs is the strangest and most dangerous (Deleuze and Guattari 1987, 163). It occurs with too much sedimentation, the selection of homogenous matter from a subordinate flow, and the deposition of these materials into layers (1987, 40–45). The matter that is sedimented is affective-cognitive chunks of desire desiring its own repression: the desire to command and be commanded, the desire to have everything in its place. The result here is a cancer of the stratum, a proliferation of points of capture, a proliferation of micro–black holes or hard subjects. Thousands of individuals, complete unto themselves. Legislators and subjects all in one. Judge, jury, and executioner—and policeman, private eye, home video operator, Neighborhood Watch organizer. . . . Watching over themselves as much as over others in runaway conscience-formation. Deleuze and Guattari call this situation "micro-fascism" (1987, 228). Here we could pick up the analyses of Klaus Theweleit in *Male Fantasies* (1987–89): microfascism desires the hard, armored body that keeps flows carefully channeled except in the fury of combat when the enemy—whose flows and organ couplings enrage the fascist—can be turned into the "bloody mass." See Connolly (2017) for a recent reading of Theweleit.

Deleuze and Guattari distinguish molecular fascism from molar totalitarianism. They name points for historical investigation of molecular or microfascism as "molecular focuses in interaction . . . rural fascism and city or neighborhood fascism, youth fascism and war veteran's fascism, fascism of the Left and of the Right, fascism of the couple, family, school, and office" (1987, 214). "Molecular" here means a population seen in terms of local interactions; molar is a population seen by reference to a standard measure. "Masses"—which are not equivalent to Canetti's sense of a "crowd" magnetized by a leader—are molecular, they always leak out from the molar "classes" that "crystallize" them. So microfascism is a molecular spread throughout a social fabric prior to the centralizing resonance that creates the molar state apparatus. Deleuze and Guattari describe microfascism as a proliferation of tiny centers of command; each body is a "micro–black hole that stands on its own and communicates with the others" (228).

Let us put such "communicating" in terms of Gabriel Tarde's microsociology (1903), whose elementary unit is the modification of a subject's beliefs and desires (in my terms, affective-cognitive structures) by imitation, opposition, or invention that constitutes waves or flows. These desire flows get "sedimented" in rates too high to be "overcoded" by traditional meaning systems. I would like here to give a Tardean reading of the case study by William Sheridan Allen, *The Nazi Seizure of Power (2014)*. For Allen, it wasn't so much the effects of the Depression that started the radicalization of the petty bourgeoisie of Northeim as "the fear of its continued effects" (Allen 2014, 24). While the reduction of credit directly and economically hurt workers, the uncertainty of the valence of the libidinal investment of credit flows set up the propagation of fear: "the rest of the townspeople, haunted by the tense faces of the unemployed, asked themselves, 'Am I next?' 'When will it end?'" Because there were no clear answers desperation grew" (24–25). It is in the midst of these affective waves of fear and desperation that Nazi energy and dedication cut an attractive figure in Northeim in early 1930: "To the average Northeimer the Nazis appeared vigorous, dedicated, and young" (32).

Such communication between "a thousand little monomanias, self-evident truths, and clarities" creates a sort of static, which inhibits state resonance by a kind of "rumble and buzz, blinding lights giving any and everybody the mission of self-appointed judge, dispenser of justice, policeman, neighborhood SS man" (Deleuze and Guattari 1987, 228). This static of microfascism keeps it below the level of the state: a thousand independent and self-appointed policemen do not make a Gestapo, though they may be a necessary condition for one. Although Deleuze and Guattari do not do so, we can call microfascism "molecular molarity": each unit is self-contained, oriented to unity, an individual (molar), but they interact in solely local manner, independently (molecular).

Microfascism is defined as the state of a social fabric "when a *war machine* is installed in each hole, in every niche" (1987, 214; italics in original). War machines are not unorganized; it is just that they are not organismically organized for the benefit of a despot: their leaders are ad hoc and challengeable, rather than reified and deified. War machines occupy and extend "smooth space," a form of spatial organization that is locally dense and flexible rather than homogenous and pre-demarcated, as in the gridded or striated space established by states. In smooth space, a law of distance disperses figures across a zone; in striated space, the space is demarcated prior to occupation, and figures are assigned to marked spots. War machines are thus the key to creation, to mutation in an open future. They constantly throw off lines of flight that move systems off territorial bindings and away from coded behavior. A war machine is a way of organizing social production that prevents the formation of a socius. In concrete terms, this means the war machine wards off capture by a state by occupying the smooth space of immanent relations.

The "third danger" of social life, according to Deleuze and Guattari, is "Power," such as when a state captures a war machine and turns it into its armed forces. The "fourth danger" is worse, however; it happens when a war machine takes over a state and posits war and war alone as its object. This is the "great Disgust, the longing to kill and die, the Passion for abolition" (227). The fourth and greatest danger is the danger of the lines of flight themselves, which "emanate a strange despair, like an odor of death and immolation, a state of war from which one returns broken" (229). Here we find the war machine, the concrete machinic assemblage of mutation, social immanence, failing at mutation: "war is like the fall or failure of mutation" (230). Here we find the analogue of the suicidal, empty BwO in a fascist war machine that has mobilized an incipient microfascist social fabric to take over the state and has thereby found, suicidally, nothing but war as its object. Both suicides—the empty BwO and the fascist state—are nihilistic, both tend to zero but on different trajectories: one direct and depressive, the other indirectly, after a manic ascension into a war frenzy. Such fascist suicidal nihilism is qualitatively different from a freezing, reflective, depressive, "lunar" nihilism that sinks relentlessly and entropically to zero; rather, fascist nihilism is a frantic, "solar" nihilism, which burns out to zero on a trajectory through a superintensity of heat produced by its own manic motion, its fascinated pursuit of war.

### Can We Save Ideology by Including Affect?

We have noted the need to account for the capacity to participate in punishment practices that constitute coercive reproduction. And that aspect needs to have an account of affect constitutive of concrete mental states since torture and killing (by nonpsychopaths) requires overriding at least some level of inhibition produced by empathic identification with a subject in pain, even given attenuation of empathy across group lines.

The relations among empathy, arousal, and violence are complex, and the literature discussing them is massive and constantly evolving. Nonetheless, some outlines can be observed: increasing in-group empathy increases the violence of punishment of out-group members for threats to in-group, and the targets of that violence receive less empathic resonance with the punishers, resulting in lower estimations of the pain dealt out. However, there must still be some recognition of pain in the targets, or else the notion of punishment loses its sense: you do not torture a wall, even if you bang on it out of frustration. So, despite the attenuation of empathy toward out-group members, consistent testimony from combatants shows the strong emotional surge necessary for almost all people to engage in violent confrontation. The question of desensitization is also difficult; one might think experience in violence, by desensitization, would ease the barriers to the engagement in violence, but burnout is also possible, such that it is sometimes newcomers who are more likely to engage in violent activity, though sometimes, due to their freshness, the results of witnessing the carnage can be emotionally devastating to them.

The tension of the group face-off characteristic of much combat, however, once broken, can result in routs and torture of the enemy, especially in a situation in which a helpless enemy faces a group; in this case, the conquering group members can escalate the atrocities in a lateral display to their comrades. While the heavy racial inflection of the use of torture of slaves in the United States as elements of coercive social reproduction would require some modification of this basic schema, I think it's clear that a strong affective component is necessary for that practice. (One of the best works on the social psychology of violence I know, and the study of which is the source from which I draw most of these remarks, is Collins 2008)

To get to "affective ideology," we have to distinguish between belief-desire psychology as a philosophical explanation of behavior and the psychological processes involved in the encoding of experiential regularities. This absorption or enculturation mode of ideology transmission accords with research done on unconscious transmission of racial bias via body comportment independent of the semantic content of accompanying words (Castelli, De Dea, and Nesdale 2008). We could also note here Susanna Siegel's work on perception in which gaze following indicates confidence, thus indicating a pattern of social valuation (cited in Stanley 2015, 249).

Jason Stanley, in *How Propaganda Works* (2015), holds that behavior-explanatory beliefs are generated from regularities of experience. I take it to be a widely accepted psychological fact that the experiential encoding of regularities is going to encode the affective tone of the situation along with representations of state of the world. From the perspective of experiential encoding, emotions aren't separate mental states that bind beliefs to agents; they are an inherent part of the experience and become associated with the representational content.

Hence the emotions produced in the scenes of daily life are part of what is transmitted by the identity-constituting practices: the reproduction of the practice of white supremacy for a slave-holding family (to use Stanley's example) is not simply accounted for by instilling in children beliefs with the propositional content of racial superiority and inferiority and binding them to those identities by love for friends and parents who participate in that practice. The reproduction of the practice of white supremacy is also constituted by an affective structure of white pride and vengeance motivated by white vulnerability, and hatred, fear, and contempt for blacks that is encoded along with the representational content of the scenes of humiliation, torture, and death that constitute the daily practices of the coercive reproduction side of plantation white supremacy (see Baptist 2014 for claims that widespread torture was responsible for increased productivity on cotton plantations). As the actions constituting the punishment practices have heavy affective components, both for active, immediate participants and for family members who experience the scenes of torture, the affective disposition allowing gruesome torture has to be part of the ideological transmission.

To conclude, if we restrict ideology critique to identifying cognitive errors (category mistakes and false empirical generalizations as generating bad beliefs, and confirmation bias and resistance to rational revision of beliefs as keeping them in place) then we risk missing an essential component of unjust social systems: the production of emotional commitments that accompany those beliefs and that allow for the punishment on which part of the effectiveness of coercive reproduction rests. But if we push too far into the affective at the expense of the cognitive, are we really talking about "ideology" anymore?

Throwing away the cognitive component of ideology critique seems too much; some people, sometimes, do respond to a cognitively oriented ideology critique: they are open to persuasion via exhibition of their cognitive errors; their beliefs become rationally revisable. However, that seems only to happen after a change in social identities—a move to a new location, the gaining of new friends—and that change has an affective component.

So, I think we should retain the term "ideology" but broaden its scope to include the affective as well as the cognitive. Our concrete lives as "bodies politic" integrate the cognitive and the affective, and recognizing that is needed to account for both coercive reproduction and for the occasionally successful rational revision of beliefs via ideology critique.

# Conclusion: Human Nature at the Edges of the State

> Human infants as young as 14 to 18 months of age help others attain their goals, for example, by helping them to fetch out-of-reach objects or opening cabinets for them. They do this irrespective of any reward from adults (indeed external rewards undermine the tendency), and very likely with no concern for such things as reciprocation and reputation, which serve to maintain altruism in older children and adults.
>
> —WARNEKEN AND TOMASELLO, "The Roots of Human Altruism"

IF WE ACCEPT that "prosociality" is the default setting for human nature, then the following is an ethical standard that finds support in an evolutionary account of human nature: *act such that you nurture the capacity to enact repeatable active joyous encounters of positive sympathetic care and fair cooperation for self and others without qualification.*

This is an exhortation to a way of life rather than full-fledged moral imperative; hermits and misanthropes are not necessarily immoral but they are not living as well as they could be. It is also just a first-order account; I will not enter into meta-ethical territory, and I am leaving the principle's relation to law making to one side. (The dark mirror of altruism is psychopathy, so the political theory question of security from social predators—what Kant in "Perpetual Peace" [1991] calls making a state that would work for a "race of devils"—is beyond what I can do here, but suffice it to say that the problem is real. Having sympathetic care and fair cooperation be the default setting doesn't mean disarming ourselves. In addition to Sen 1977, see Hirstein and Sifferd 2014.) I can say that whatever your principle of moral judgment, a grasp of evolved human nature is important for your moral pedagogy, how to get to where we should be from where we are. Furthermore, I avoid the naturalistic fallacy in that I do not claim my standard is correct because it is grounded in evolved human nature. But I do think showing that evolved human nature is congruent with that standard is a needed intervention in contemporary debates in philosophy, anthropology, and psychology.

Human nature is a multiplicity, a virtual differential field of bio-neuro-cultural processes insisting in different existing actual assemblages of prosocial, politically inflected, affective cognition. Each person is an assemblage differently incarnating that pattern: we are all solutions to the problem "how to be human?" Rather than being essentialist or teleological—in which one concrete form effaces itself in its guise of a universal—the human nature concept here can only be nomological (Machery 2008), describing general outcomes for most people under loosely defined environmental situations, and without pejorative boundary setting for those whose performance is atypical (psychopaths are human beings, after all). Prosociality means a primary orientation to sympathetic care and fair cooperation, which is nonetheless admitting of rational, egoist-driven violence and competition under duress. Furthermore, with certain territorialization processes—perhaps beginning with herding, but certainly accelerating with states and grain agriculture—prosociality comes with a gradient favoring the in-group.

This notion of human nature as a multiplicity of biocultural processes with differenciating singular outcomes resonates with Sylvia Wynter's "sociogenic principle" (Wynter 2001). Wynter invokes a deep plasticity whereby social patterns of experience use biological capacities for targeted release of neurotransmitters to produce feeling structures. Wynter takes her cue from Fanon's analysis of how "black skins" are overlain by "white masks" and how the pathologies of colonialism can become deeply embodied as "cortico-visceral illnesses" in both colonizer and colonized. Socializing practices also enter into complex feedback relations with the singular body makeup of the people involved. (I wrote *Political Affect* before I came across Wynter, but there I sketch out Iris Marion Young's analysis of the corporealization of femininity in "Throwing Like a Girl" and describe a multiplicity of intersecting corporealization practices producing a field of "bodies politic.")

To repeat, then, evolved human nature is a multiplicity of bio-neuro-cultural processes producing different individuals with different patterns of "prosocial, politically inflected affective cognition." The range of those differences—all formally prosocial but with different content—comes from our plasticity.

Our early hominin ancestors encountered a highly variable environment necessitating collaboration. Counterintuitively—but why do we have *this* intuition?—the world was too dangerous to afford competition, let alone war. We therefore evolved toward great plasticity of intelligent behavior to the extent that we engage in "niche construction": we change our environment so that it could be inherited in predictable ways but never so rigidly as to disallow cultural change.

Together, then, plasticity and niche construction mean humans have evolved so that most are open to prosocialization processes. "Prosocialization" entails being evolutionarily prepared to be intellectually and emotionally invested in, though never determined by, the social and somatic patterns we inhabit and that guide our caring and cooperative relations—and even our violent and competitive relations—with those around us. Cultural accrual is not naively progressivist, however; many cultures produce vastly unequal distributions of costs and benefits, very often intertwined, as we have hinted, with gender and race distinctions. Some even reach the point where we emotionally invest in being dominated. As Spinoza put it, sometimes we fight for our domination as if it were our salvation. This is the problem of fascist desire, the desire to have command and obedience be the sole form of human relation.

I also hasten to say that when those social patterns conflict, moral reflection and collaborative discussion can and should intervene—and they conflict quite often, even in forager band societies earlier generations would have characterized as "simple." Humans have been arguing about what is the right thing to do for a very long time; we are "political animals" even before or outside the restricted sense of "polis" as city; in fact, I'd say there's more political and moral reflection and discussion in "simple" egalitarian forager bands than in the households and imperial courts of "complex" hierarchical situations, where commands are issued and obeyed or resisted. We could say that prosocialization is always fracturing and being repaired with both affective and cognitive remediation qua sympathetic care and moral argument.

But now to deal with the elephant in the room: the "gradient" of prosociality at the boundary of the group, such that we tend to put social group "qualifications" on our care and cooperation. Recall that Bergson (1977), for one, doubts whether prosocial tendencies, which he associates with the "closed society," could ever be expanded; it might be that a leap into another regime of political affect, an "open society" regime, is required (Lawlor 2018).

Because of this, the moral pedagogy needed to meet the "without qualification" portion of this normative standard is not easy. But at least we can say that in trying to get people to enact repeatable active joyous encounters for self and others "without qualification" we are working to arrange social life to expand the scope of a basic orientation of human nature for care and cooperation and not, *pace* Huxley ("Darwin's Bulldog") and the 150 years of people in his wake, trying to intensify a mere cultural constraint on a deep and primary natural impulse to violent competition within and across groups (e.g., Wrangham 1999).

This is not, by the way, the problem with Steven Pinker's *Better Angels of Our Nature* (2011), which clearly denies a basic violence drive and instead insists that we have both peaceful and violent capacities that are elicited by social circumstances. And as a good modern liberal, I endorse the changing social circumstances of mobility, cosmopolitanism, revisionist history, and so on that, per Pinker's hypothesis, led to an uptick in moral investment in fairness and respect for individuals versus old-fashioned takes on communal loyalty, authority, and purity. Rather, my issue with him is his acceptance of the Chimpanzee Referential Doctrine so that the social eliciting of altruism is always scrambling to catch up with what used to be a violence orientation to our evolutionary ancestors. This results in a model in which top-down and outside-in ("internalized norms against violence") rational, frontal-lobe self-control (the most important of "our better angels") keeps limbic system emotional temptations to violence ("our inner demons") in check. That's fine as far as it goes, but for the most part his treatment of our better angels, although it does include empathy/sympathy, doesn't really analyze bottom-up, limbic-based emotional dispositions to sympathetic care and fair cooperation. This is compounded with other problems with Pinker: (1) his questionable methods in his analyses of pre-state violence (Ferguson 2013a and 2013b), contemporary nonstate violence, and contemporary state violence (not just death rates in war narrowly considered but war widely considered [e.g., influenza after World War I], and the fate of condemnation to hidden slavery sweatshops and to being despair-ridden "losers" leading lives worse than death; and (2) the restricted political space in which Pinker's Western Civilization Whig story operates.

In a way, I am arguing for Kropotkin rather than Huxley as the true heir to Darwin: natural selection, especially in human beings, operates via cooperation and competition, not just competition; struggling cooperatively with your group *and with other groups* against environmental forces and not just struggling competitively within the group and across groups for scarce resources. We have that capacity for violent intragroup competition, of course, as history sadly attests (inflamed *amour propre* in which injury becomes insult is a dangerous sentiment indeed). But the postulated violence within early human groups is exaggerated; i.e., it follows a questionably "chimpocentric" view of humans, as some recent work suggests (Vaesen 2014; Gonzalez-Cabrera 2017).

As for intergroup competition, a strong "in-group/out-group" distinction is arguably not reflective of the early evolutionary setting for humans, where fission-fusion in the unsegmented forager band way of life, and the relative advantage of making allies when the spoils of conquest were so meager and the defensive advantage so great (Kelly 2005; Sterelny 2014), meant porosity of boundaries rather than strong borders (Casey 2017). This is the condition for cultural diffusion via trade and imitation, as group members are always going back and forth. Even for Bergson (1977), the "closed society" is a tendency rather than a chronological posit. This is our opening to insist that any group—even "primitive." to use Bergson's outdated terminology—includes potential for peaceful collaboration and alliance with outsiders from the start.

So, my bottom line here: our ancestors did indeed develop ways to detect and punish bullies and shirkers and so to suppress our dominance-enabling, hair-trigger temper and violent reactive aggression, as in the Human Self-Domestication hypothesis. But, contra Gaus (2015), foragers do not settle for cooperation simply out of the fear that not cooperating would unleash the bullies and shirkers that lurk within all of us. Rather, they also genuinely and positively developed an emotional structure that can motivate us, their descendants, to search for the joy we directly find in cooperation, sharing, and helping.

# Acknowledgments

My students in courses offered in the Roger Hadfield Ogden Honors College at Louisiana State University, as well as in the Department of French Studies and the Department of Philosophy & Religious Studies, have helped me refine my thinking here. I'd also like to acknowledge Grant McCall, Karl Widerquist, Brian Marks, Kent Mathewson, and Helen Regis for help with anthropology and geography questions. Talks delivered at the following association meetings also helped with the genesis of this book: American Political Science Association; American Association of Geographers; Society for Literature, Science, and the Arts; International Studies Association; Society for Phenomenology and Existential Philosophy; and Society for European Philosophy (UK). Similarly, invited talks at the following universities were instrumental in formulating this book: Stony Brook University; American University in Paris; Radboud University; Institute for Arts & Humanities at Penn State University; the CIEPFC seminar at the Ecole Normale Supérieure; Notre Dame University; Elmhurst College; Clemson University; Duquesne University; University of Memphis; University of Hawai'i at Manoa; and University of Dundee.

# Works Cited

Allen, William Sheridan. 2014 (1965). *The Nazi Seizure of Power*. Brattleboro, Vt.: Echo Point Books & Media.

Baptist, Edward. 2014. *The Half Has Never Been Told: Slavery and the Making of American Capitalism*. New York: Basic Books.

Barrett, Lisa Feldman. 2017. *How Emotions Are Made: The Secret Life of the Brain*. New York: Harcourt Mifflin.

Barrett, Louise. 2011. *Beyond the Brain: How Body and Environment Shape Animal and Human Minds*. Princeton, N.J.: Princeton University Press.

Bergson, Henri. 1977 (1935). *The Two Sources of Morality and Religion*. Trans. R. Ashley Audra, Cloudsley Brereton, and W. Horsfall Carter. Notre Dame, Ind.: University of Notre Dame Press.

Boehm, Christopher. 2012a. "Ancestral Hierarchy and Conflict." *Science* 336 (6083): 844–47.

Boehm, Christopher. 2012b. *Moral Origins: The Evolution of Virtue, Altruism, and Shame*. New York: Basic Books.

Bowles, Samuel and Herbert Gintis. 2011. *A Cooperative Species: Human Reciprocity and Its Evolution*. Princeton, N.J.: Princeton University Press.

Casey, Edward S. 2017. *The World on Edge*. Bloomington: Indiana University Press.

Castelli, L., C. De Dea, and D. Nesdale. 2008. "Learning Social Attitudes: Children's Sensitivity to the Nonverbal Behaviors of Adult Models during Interracial Interactions." *Personality and Social Psychology Bulletin* 34, no. 11: 1504–13.

Chagnon, Napoleon. 1988. "Life Histories, Blood Revenge, and Warfare in a Tribal Population." *Science* 318:636–40.

Clastres, Pierre. 1989. *Society against the State*. Trans. Robert Hurley and Abe Stein. New York: Zone Books.

Clastres, Pierre. 1994. *Archaeology of Violence*. Trans. Jeanine Herman. New York: Semiotext(e).

CNN. 2010. "Gen. Honoré: Evacuate Most Vulnerable Haitians." http://
    www.cnn.com/2010/OPINION/01/20/honore.q.and.a/index.html.

Collins, Randall. 2008. *Violence: A Micro-sociological Theory*. Princeton,
    N.J.: Princeton University Press.

Connolly, William. 2017. *Aspirational Fascism: The Struggle for
    Multifaceted Democracy under Trumpism*. Minneapolis: University of
    Minnesota Press.

Damasio, Antonio. 1999. *The Feeling of What Happens*. New York:
    Harcourt.

Darwin, Charles. 2004 (1871). *The Descent of Man*. New York: Penguin.

Deleuze, Gilles, and Félix Guattari. 1977. *Anti-Oedipus*. Trans. R. Hurley,
    M. Seem, and H. R. Lane. Minneapolis: University of Minnesota Press.

Deleuze, Gilles, and Félix Guattari. 1987. *A Thousand Plateaus*. Trans.
    Brian Massumi. Minneapolis: University of Minnesota Press.

De Waal, Frans. 2006. *Primates and Philosophers: How Morality Evolved*.
    Princeton, N.J.: Princeton University Press.

Ferguson, Brian. 1995. *Yanomami Warfare: A Political History*. Santa Fe,
    N.M.: School for American Research Press.

Ferguson, Brian. 2008. "Ten Points on War." *Social Analysis* 52, no. 2:
    32–49.

Ferguson, Brian. 2013a. "Pinker's List: Exaggerating Prehistoric War
    Mortality." Chapter 7 in Fry 2013.

Ferguson, Brian. 2013b. "The Prehistory of War and Peace in Europe and
    the Near East." Chapter 11 in Fry 2013b.

Ferguson, Brian. 2014. "Anthropologist Finds Flaw in Claim That Chimp
    Raids Are 'Adaptive.'" http://blogs.scientificamerican.com/cross
    -check/2014/11/25/anthropologist-finds-flaw-in-claim-that-chimp
    -raids-are-adaptive/ (accessed March 28, 2015).

Foucault, Michel. 1997. *Society Must Be Defended*. Trans. David Macey.
    New York: Picador.

Foucault, Michel. 2000. *Power: The Essential Works of Foucault*. Ed. James
    Faubion. New York: New Press.

Foucault, Michel. 2008. *The Birth of Biopolitics*. Trans. Graham Burchell.
    New York: Palgrave Macmillan.

Fry, Douglas. 2007. *Beyond War: The Human Potential for Peace*. New York:
    Oxford University Press.

Fry, Douglas. 2013. "War, Peace and Human Nature: The Challenge of
    Achieving Scientific Objectivity." In *War, Peace, and Human Nature,*
    ed. Douglas Fry, 1–21. Oxford: Oxford University Press.

Fuentes, Agustín. 2013. "Cooperation, Conflict, and Niche Construction in
    the Genus *Homo*." In *War, Peace, and Human Nature,* ed. Douglas Fry,
    78–94. OxfordwOxford University Press.

Gaus, Gerald. 2015. "The Egalitarian Species." *Social Philosophy and Policy*
    31, no. 2: 1–27. doi:10.1017/S0265052514000235.

Gonzalez-Cabrera, Ivan. 2017. "On Social Tolerance and the Evolution of Human Normative Guidance." *The British Journal for the Philosophy of Science*. https://doi.org/10.1093/bjps/axx017

Gallese, Vittorio. 2001. "The 'Shared Manifold' Hypothesis: From Mirror Neurons to Empathy." *Journal of Consciousness Studies* 8, no. 5–7: 33–50.

Graeber, David. 2012. *Debt: The First 5,000 Years*. New York: Melville House.

Griffiths, Paul, and Karola Stotz. 2013. *Genetics and Philosophy*. Cambridge: Cambridge University Press.

Grossman, David. 1996. *On Killing*. Boston: Little, Brown.

Haidt, Jonathan. 2001. "The Emotional Dog and Its Rational Tail." *Psychological Review* 108, no. 4: 814–34.

Hare, Brian. 2017. "Survival of the Friendliest: Homo sapiens Evolved via Selection for Prosociality." *Annual Review of Psychology* 68:24.1–24.32

Henrich, Joseph. 2016. *The Secret of Our Success: How Culture Is Driving Human Evolution, Domesticating Our Species, and Making Us Smarter*. Princeton, N.J.: Princeton University Press.

Heyes, Cecelia. 2010. "Where Do Mirror Neurons Come From?" *Neuroscience and Biobehavioral Reviews* 34: 575–83.

Hirstein, William, and Katrina Sifferd. 2014. "Ethics and the Brains of Psychopaths: The Significance of Psychopathy for Our Ethical and Legal Theories." In *Brain Theory: Essays in Critical Neurophilosophy*, ed. Charles Wolfe, 149–70. London: Springer.

Jablonka, Eva, and Marion Lamb. 2005. *Evolution in Four Dimensions*. Cambridge Mass.: MIT Press.

Jost, J., C. Federico,, and J. Napier. 2009. "Political Ideology: Its Structure, Functions, and Elective Affinities." *Annual Review of Psychology* 60: 307–37.

Joyce, Richard. 2006. *The Evolution of Morality*. Cambridge Mass.: MIT Press.

Kant, Immanuel. 1991(1795). "Perpetual Peace: A Philosophical Sketch." In *Kant: Political Writings,* Trans. H. Nisbet, 93–130. Cambridge: Cambridge University Press.

Keeley, Lawrence. 1997. *War before Civilization: The Myth of the Peaceful Savage*. New York: Oxford University Press.

Keller, Evelyn Fox. 2000. *The Century of the Gene*. Cambridge, Mass.: Harvard University Press.

Kelly, Raymond. 2000. *Warless Societies and the Origin of War*. Ann Arbor: University of Michigan Press.

Kelly, Raymond. 2005. "The Evolution of Lethal Intergroup Violence." *Proceedings of the National Academy of Science* 102, no. 43: 15294–198. doi: 10.1073/pnas.0505955102.

Kelly, Robert L. 2013. *The Lifeways of Hunter-Gatherers: The Foraging Spectrum*. Cambridge: Cambridge University Press.

Kitcher, Philip. 2011. *The Ethical Project*. Cambridge, Mass.: Harvard University Press.

Lawlor, Leonard. 2018. "'I Value Effort above Everything Else': Bergson's Response to the Question of Egoism." *Graduate Faculty Philosophy Journal 39, no. 1: 79–101.*

LeDoux, Joseph. 1996. *The Emotional Brain*. New York: Simon and Schuster.

LeDoux, Joseph. 2016. *Anxious: Using the Brain to Understand and Treat Fear and Anxiety*. New York: Penguin.

Lévi-Strauss, Claude. 1977. "Jean-Jacques Rousseau, Founder of the Sciences of Man." In *Structural Anthropology*, vol. 2. London: Allen Lane.

Machery, Edouard. 2008. "A Plea for Human Nature." *Philosophical Psychology* 21, no. 3: 321–29.

Marks, Jonathan. 2010. *The Alternative Introduction to Biological Anthropology*. New York: Oxford University Press.

Nietzsche, Friedrich. 1997 (1887). *On the Genealogy of Morality*. Trans. Carol Diethe. Cambridge: Cambridge University Press.

Nussbaum, Martha. 1993. "Non-Relative Virtues: An Aristotelian Approach." In *The Quality of Life,* ed. Martha Nussbaum and Amartya Sen, 242–69. Oxford: Oxford University Press.

Oksala, Johanna. 2012. *Foucault, Politics, and Violence*. Evanston, Ill.: Northwestern University Press.

Ostrom, Elinor. 2005. "Policies That Crowd Out Reciprocity and Collective Action." In *Moral Sentiments and Material Interests: The Foundations of Cooperation in Economic Life,* ed. Herbert Gintis, Samuel Bowles, Robert Boyd, and Ernst Fehr, 253–75. Cambridge, Mass.: MIT Press.

Oyama, Susan, Paul Griffiths, and Russell Gray, eds. 2001. *Cycles of Contingency: Developmental Systems and Evolution*. Cambridge, Mass.: MIT Press.

Panksepp, Jaak. 1998. *Affective Neuroscience*. New York: Oxford University Press.

Pinker, Steven. 2011. *Better Angels of Our Nature: Why Violence Has Declined*. New York: Viking.

Protevi, John. 2008. "Affect, Agency, and Responsibility: The Act of Killing in the Age of Cyborgs." *Phenomenology and the Cognitive Sciences* 7, no. 2: 405–13.

Protevi, John. 2009. *Political Affect: Connecting the Social and the Somatic*. Minneapolis: University of Minnesota Press.

Protevi, John. 2013. *Life, War, Earth: Deleuze and the Sciences*. Minneapolis: University of Minnesota Press.

Protevi, John. 2016. "Foucault's Deleuzean Methodology of the Late 1970s." In *Between Deleuze and Foucault,* ed. Nicolae Morar, Thomas Nail, and Daniel Smith, 120–27. Edinburgh: Edinburgh University Press.

Protevi, John. 2018. "November 28, 1947: How Do You Make Yourself a Body without Organs?" In *A Thousand Plateaus and Philosophy,* ed, Henry Somers-Hall, Jeffrey Bell, and James Williams, 99–114. Edinburgh: Edinburgh University Press.

Reich, Wilhem. 1946. *The Mass Psychology of Fascism.* Trans. Theodore Wolfe. New York: Orgone Institute Press.

Reicher, Stephen, et al. 2007. "Knowledge-Based Public Order Policing: Principles and Practice." *Policing* 1, no. 4: 403–15. doi: 10.1093/police/pam067.

Roberts, Neil. 2015. *Freedom as Marronage.* Chicago: University of Chicago Press.

Rosen, Michael. 1996. *On Voluntary Servitude: False Consciousness and the Theory of Ideology.* Cambridge, Mass.: Harvard University Press.

Rousseau, Jean-Jacques. 1997. *Discourse on Inequality.* In *The Discourses and Other Early Political Writings,* trans. and ed., Victor Gourevitch, 111–231. Cambridge: Cambridge University Press.

Sahlins, Marshall. 1972. *Stone Age Economics.* New York: Aldine Atherton.

Scott, James C. 2009. *The Art of Not Being Governed: An Anarchist History of Upland Southeast Asia.* New Haven, Conn.: Yale University Press.

Scott, James C. 2017. *Against the Grain: A Deep History of the Earliest States.* New Haven, Conn.: Yale University Press.

Sen, Amartya. 1977. "Rational Fools: A Critique of the Behavioural Foundations of Economic Theory." *Philosophy and Public Affairs* 6, no. 4: 317–44.

Sibertin-Blanc, Guillaume. 2016. *State and Politics: Deleuze and Guattari on Marx.* Trans. Ames Hodges. New York: Semiotext(e).

Smith, Daniel. 2018. "7000BC: Apparatus of Capture." In *A Thousand Plateaus and Philosophy,* ed, Henry Somers-Hall, Jeffrey Bell, and James Williams, 223–41. Edinburgh: Edinburgh University Press.

Sober, Elliott, and David Sloan Wilson. 1998. *Unto Others: The Evolution and Psychology of Unselfish Behavior.* Cambridge, Mass.: Harvard University Press.

Spinoza, Benedict. 2002. *Spinoza: The Collected Works.* Trans. Samuel Shirley, ed. Michael L. Morgan. Indianapolis: Hackett.

Stanley, Jason. 2015. *How Propaganda Works.* Princeton, N.J.: Princeton University Press.

Sterelny, Kim. 2012. *The Evolved Apprentice: How Evolution Made Humans Unique.* Cambridge, Mass.: MIT Press.

Sterelny, Kim. 2014. "Cooperation, Culture, and Conflict." *British Journal for the Philosophy of Science* 67, no. 1: 1–28.

Stueber, Karsten. 2017. "Empathy." In *The Stanford Encyclopedia of Philosophy,* ed., Edward N. Zalta, https://plato.stanford.edu/archives/spr2017/entries/empathy/.

Tarde, Gabriel. 1903. *The Laws of Imitation.* Trans. Elsie Clews Parsons. New York: Henry Holt.

Theweleit, Klaus. 1987–89. *Male Fantasies.* 2 vols. Minneapolis: University of Minnesota Press

Tierney, Kathleen, Christine Bevc, and Erica Kuligowski. 2006. "Metaphors Matter: Disaster Myths, Media Frames, and Their Consequences in Hurricane Katrina." *Annals of the American Academy of Social and Political Science* 604, no. 1: 57–81.

Tomasello, Michael. 2009. *Why We Cooperate.* Cambridge, Mass.: MIT Press.

Tomasello, Michael. 2016. *A Natural History of Human Morality.* Cambridge, Mass.: Harvard University Press.

Vaesen, Krist. 2014. "Chimpocentrism and Reconstructions of Human Evolution (A Timely Reminder)." *Studies in History and Philosophy of Biological and Biomedical Sciences* 45:12–21.

Warneken, Felix, and Michael Tomasello. 2008. "Extrinsic Rewards Undermine Altruistic Tendencies in 20-Month-Olds." *Developmental Psychology* 44, no. 6: 1785–88.

Welsch, Robert, Luis Vivanco, and Agustín Fuentes. 2017. *Anthropology: Asking Questions about Human Origins, Diversity, and Culture.* New York: Oxford University Press.

Wexler, Bruce. 2006. *Brain and Culture: Neurobiology, Ideology, and Social Change.* Cambridge, Mass.: MIT Press.

Widerquist, Karl, and Grant McCall. 2017. *Prehistoric Myths in Modern Political Philosophy.* Edinburgh: Edinburgh University Press.

Wittfogel, Karl. 1957. *Oriental Despotism: A Comparative Study of Total Power.* New Haven, Conn.: Yale University Press.

Wokler, Robert. 2012. "Perfectible Apes in Decadent Cultures: Rousseau's Anthropology Revisited." In *Rousseau, the Age of Enlightenment, and Their Legacies,* 1–28. Princeton, N.J.: Princeton University Press.

Wrangham, Richard. 1999. "Evolution of Coalitionary Killing." *American Journal of Physical Anthropology* 110 (Supplement 29): 1–30.

Wrangham, Richard. 2009. *Catching Fire: How Cooking Made Us Human.* New York: Basic Books.

Wrangham, Richard. 2014. *Did Homo Sapiens Self-Domesticate?* http:// www.uctv.tv/shows/CARTA-Domestication-and-Human-Evolution -Richard-Wrangham-Did-Homo-Sapiens-Self-Domesticate-28902.

Wrangham, Richard, and Dale Peterson. 1996. *Demonic Males: Apes and the Origins of Human Violence.* New York: Houghton Mifflin.

Wynter, Sylvia. 2001. "Towards the Sociogenic Principle: Fanon, Identity, the Puzzle of Conscious Experience, and What It Is Like to Be 'Black.'" In *National Identities and Sociopolitical Changes in Latin America,* ed. Mercedes F Durán-Cogan and Antonio Gómez-Moriana, 30–66. New York: Routledge.

**John Protevi** is Phyllis M. Taylor Professor of French Studies and professor of philosophy at Louisiana State University. He is author of *Political Affect* (Minnesota, 2009) and *Life, War, Earth* (Minnesota, 2013) and editor of *A Dictionary of Continental Philosophy.*

Lightning Source UK Ltd.
Milton Keynes UK
UKHW010104290319
340124UK00001B/48/P